PRAISE FOR FUTURE-PROOF YOUR BRAND

" In an era of Digital Darwinism, branding is key. It's all about organisations that manage to be agile and adaptive. Gut feeling can help, but strong in-depth knowledge about branding and the ability to adapt is the foundation for success. Within this excellent book, Laurens and Marc prove that looking at branding from the business administration side is crucial for future brand performance. A must read for every board."

John van der Ent, Chairman Papendal Holding, Boardroom Advisor, former CEO, V&D/La Place Group

" *Future-Proof Your Brand* shows in a thought-provocative way why brands matter in creating and, above all, protecting competitive advantage of a firm. A must read for professionals in communication and branding."

Dr. Cees B.M. van Riel, Professor of Corporate Communication, Rotterdam School of Management/Erasmus University Rotterdam

" Having worked with Marc and Laurens for several years, I have noted that they are very well positioned to support leading, mostly global brands in realising that international brand value is a key item in enterprise value. They support, both on a strategic as well as operational hands-on level, their clients in this process, with specific focus on rebranding exercises."

Rob van der Laan, Managing Partner, NewPort Capital

❝ I am absolutely impressed by the deep dive both branding experts Marc and Laurens did in the world of repositioning organisations and firms. The brand and brand value is, in todays fast-changing economic environment, far beyond creativity, design, colors and logos. It's all about in-depth knowledge and 'reading' the specific environment, the vision, mission, the products and shared beliefs of the entire organisation. And that's what they are doing as bright listeners and straightforward creative sparring partners that are pretty hands-on in the transition.

For me this book is a challenging must-read for every Chief Marketing Officer and CEO facing tough weather!"

Frans van Steenis, CEO, Nederlandse Staatsloterij, former Managing Partner, Deloitte

❝ This book shows that the brands of the future are the ones that succeed in leveraging brand equity with technology. That makes brand management, per definition, a boardroom topic and far too important to be just left to the marketing department.

Marc and Laurens show that managing your brand is a profession that, if done well, is crucial for the future of the organisation."

Nanne Bos, Global Head of Brand Management, ING Group

FUTURE PROOF YOUR BRAND

DATA-DRIVEN INSIGHTS TO IMPLEMENT, MANAGE, AND OPTIMISE YOUR BRAND PERFORMANCE

FOREWORDS BY KARL-LUDWIG KLEY AND RALPH HAMERS

MARC CLOOSTERMAN | LAURENS HOEKSTRA

ISBN 978-0-9990823-0-0

REBRAND Publishing™
Published 2017 I First printing
Published simultaneously in electronic format

24 Corliss Street No. 6791
Providence, RI 02940 USA

Printed in the United States of America
Printed by Meridian Printing

Connect with VIM Group: vim-group.com I @vim_group
Connect with REBRAND: REBRAND.com I @REBRANDing

REBRAND.

Transform to Thrive™

Where the world goes for winning brands.

We publish, showcase, and advise C-suite experts
and global leaders driving and transforming brands.

"A relevant and differentiating identity is a condition for a strong reputation and sustainable success. It creates competitive advantage, contributes to profitability, and is both an enabler and success factor for constructive change."

Ralph Hamers
CEO and Chairman
Executive Board, ING Group

ACKNOWLEDGMENTS

Before you start your journey of reading this book, we would like to express our sincere gratitude to those that have helped us get to where we are today. First and foremost, we thank both our wives Ceciel and Marieke, as well as our children, for having such patience with us over the last year. Next, we thank Rene Kroeze, our trusted partner in business.

It's one thing to play with the idea that we should write down and share our experiences, but a totally different thing to get it done. And yet, we're utterly grateful to have embarked on this journey.

Our company's founders, Bert Nijboer and Eric Nijkamp, started their company NykampNyboer in 1991 based on their belief that brand implementation was a profession, one that required specialisation, in order to unleash the magic of brands to their full potential. And today, this is still our core belief.

They created a new category within branding: brand implementation and management. Thanks to their pioneering efforts, we've been able to expand this business globally to become the leading brand implementation and management firm.

As founders of the category, we deem it our duty to now share our insights and best practices. And this is why we've gone through the demanding process of creating this book for you.

We owe a huge thanks to all of our family and friends for their sacrifice of having seen us even less whilst we worked on this book.

Marc Cloosterman   Laurens Hoekstra

We also thank our talented VIM Group team for their invaluable support, contributions, and expertise in the creation of this book.

Roz Bacon	Amanda Groeneveld	Anoek Pattiasina
Niels Beemink	Thijs Hardeman	Jos Rake
Rene Bekker	Cassie Healey	Frederik Rutgers
Bjorn Bekkers	Ivar Hannessen	Diederik Sas
Mathieu Blenke	Esmé Hilgeholt	Melissa Stroobach
Marc Bles	Ard van den Hoek	Marlon Versteeg
Wendy Bolhuis	Sander Hoepman	Erik Voskuijl
Cristina Calvo	Marco Hofman	Thijs Weggeman
Jo Davies	Garfield Johns	Julian Thomas
Edwin aan de Stegge	Andreas Korwes	Rik Weideman
Richard de Luca	Rene Kroeze	Margôt Westerhof
Jos Diender	Jim Krokké	Tammo Westra
Cor van Dronkelaar	Stephan Laarhuis	Helen Wildvank
Michel van Eijnatten	Wieke Lenderink	Cat Wise
Niek Fransen	Jort Mentink	Bert Wolters
Michael Gentle	Robin Mentink	Muhammer Yilmaz

CONTENTS

2   PREFACE

4   FOREWORDS BY KARL-LUDWIG KLEY AND RALPH HAMERS

8   **PART 1** | WELCOME TO THE FUTURE OF YOUR BUSINESS

28   **PART 2** | BRAND PERFORMANCE STRATEGY FOR THE C-SUITE

78   **PART 3** | BRAND CHANGE AND MANAGEMENT THAT DRIVES ROI

118   **PART 4** | LEARNING FROM EXAMPLES

128   **PART 5** | FAQS: ASKING AND ANSWERING THE RIGHT QUESTIONS

153   RESOURCES

154   REFERENCES

157   ABOUT THE AUTHORS

161   ABOUT VIM GROUP

PREFACE

This book is a collection of our methods for solving brand implementation and management challenges.

Our purpose at the outset was focused. Brands are organisations' most important intangible assets, and their management is absolutely critical. Traditionally, brands have been created by agencies, and brand management has been undervalued. Fortunately, that mindset is now shifting, and we are pleased to have been part of the effort to build awareness about the value of brands.

Our goal for *Future-Proof Your Brand* is to help you deliver and manage brand change. From our twenty-five-plus years of experience, we have found that smart integration of data-driven insights, mission-critical logistics, and predictive analytics for future change make that delivery and management possible and successful.

We began with a deep understanding that strong brands drive competitive advantage and shareholder value. Research by respected organisations such as Brand Finance, supports this fact. Brands are built from the inside out, helping you recruit and keep the best employees who are essential to your marketplace success.

We then developed proprietary processes that have achieved results for 1200-plus organisations around the globe. Some of those include SkyTeam, Deutsche Telekom, Merck, Airbus Group, and ING Group. Our straightforward processes facilitate decisions that impact your employees, customers, and prospects.

The top concerns of your board and C-suite are usually questions about costs, timing, and ROI. We address these concerns to help you move forward with confidence. This book is a collection of our methods for solving brand implementation and management challenges. It covers the essentials and more. We tried to make the concepts, tools, and recommended steps specific and digestible. We have provided case examples, articles, tools, and our experienced work methodologies, as well as answers to questions we frequently receive.

But the support doesn't stop there. We have also compiled an evolving resource at our website to help you plan, deliver, and manage your brand change. Choosing aspects you need from *Future-Proof Your Brand* and putting them into practice will help you achieve your desired results.

Effective brand transformations demand experienced professionals with a proven track record to deliver, manage, and evolve brand assets successfully. As the world's leading brand implementation firm, we are proud to be an ongoing business partner for organisations in times of change.

FOREWORD KARL-LUDWIG KLEY

Business is global. Despite current attempts by some politicians to reset the wheel of economics to its national starting position, there is no way of getting around the normative power of the present state, otherwise known as globalisation. Digitalisation and Industry 4.0 are driving the global economy at an unprecedented pace. Consequently, companies are no longer just competing on a regional or national level. Competition is coming from all sides, and has intensified. Products and services are becoming increasingly interchangeable, and the battle to attract the best talent has become fierce.

For companies, it is more important than ever to have a strong reputation and to uniquely position themselves in the marketplace. Who are we, what do we stand for, what sets us apart from the competition? Those unable to answer these questions run the risk of making themselves irrelevant. Or they will simply fail to be heard in the cacophony of global communication. A strong company brand is thus not just another nice-to-have element that manifests itself in good rankings. A strong company brand is essential for business success.

As such, the brand is far more than just a logo. Those who dismiss brand management as a mere interplay of colors and shapes underestimate its significance— and thus miss opportunities for their corporation. A compelling corporate design is of course the most visible expression of a brand. However, if it is not based on an equally convincing communications and marketing strategy that appeals to customers, employees and applicants alike, and has not been developed from nor aligned with the company's strategy, a lot of money could end up being spent on a stylish but ultimately insubstantial new design.

> A strong company brand is essential for business success

In addition, brands must be developed over the long term if they are to generate the desired success in keeping with corporate strategy. This requires more than a fresh coat of paint every few years. It requires clearly defined messages, as well as an organisation that is willing and able to put its horsepower on the road, also in an environment characterised by resource efficiency and KPIs.

Ultimately, successful brands need both the creativity of the designer, who is able to transform an abstract brand idea into a world of images, and the rationality of a brand strategist, who can not only develop sustainable brand models, but can also anchor brand management as a value-adding element of the company. If the two come together, then companies will be equipped to make a visible mark—their visible mark—on the global stage.

Karl-Ludwig Kley
Chairman of the Supervisory Board of E.ON

Former Chairman of the Executive Board of Merck

Karl-Ludwig Kley is Chairman of the Supervisory Board of energy supplier E.ON. In 1982, he began his career with Bayer, where he initially worked in Corporate Finance and later became assistant to the Chairman of the Management Board. He was Chief Financial Officer of Bayer in Japan, Head of the Pharmaceutical division of Bayer's Italian subsidiary and later served as Head of Finance and Investor Relations of Bayer. From 1998 to 2006, Karl-Ludwig Kley was Chief Financial Officer of Lufthansa, before joining Merck as Vice Chairman of the Executive Board. From 2007 to 2016, he was Chairman of the Executive Board and CEO of Merck.

FOREWORD RALPH HAMERS

We are living through an era of unprecedented change. Change is all around us. Needs change, markets change, technology changes—and as a result, people and organisations have to change. In recent years, many industries have been hard hit by a vicious combination of disruptive pressures: recession, changing consumer behaviour, exponentially more powerful digital technologies, increased out-of-sector competition, and the emergence of new innovative business models. But change can be both positive and necessary. Without change, businesses would likely lose their competitive edge and fail to meet the needs and expectations of their loyal customers.

As technology embeds itself deeply into every aspect of our lives, it's crucial that brands learn how to quickly adapt and adjust while staying true to their identities. A clear identity has the power to engage customers, employees and all other stakeholders. A clear identity has the power to align all functions of the organisation. In this context, the brand becomes a reference point that connects, engages, and brings purpose and meaning. This is a relatively new role for brands, but an increasingly important one, because a relevant and differentiating identity is a condition for a strong reputation and sustainable success. It creates competitive advantage, contributes to profitability, and is both an enabler and success factor for constructive change.

ING began its transformation journey in 2013, with a new strategy: Think Forward. Our brand purpose is central to this strategy, and guides us in exploring new ways of delivering on our promise to customers: to always be clear and easy, always available, continuously improving, and most of all, to empower people in life and business.

It also guides us in how we can keep improving the fundamental value-creating services we provide to people, economies and society-at-large: to be a safe place for people to store their wealth, to bring together savers and borrowers, to help facilitate trade, and to drive sustainable economic growth. We do this by leveraging our brand with new technologies, connecting businesses to people and people to each other.

All this change creates great opportunities for branding professionals. But making the most of these opportunities requires hard work and focus. And it means needing to fundamentally rethink how branding professionals organise themselves, position themselves, and how they engage with the rest of the organisation. What is certain is that branding professionals need to avoid being just another cog in the marketing machine, and move themselves closer to the centre of corporate decision-making. Not to take control, because the brand is the responsibility of everyone, but to engage with all parts of the organisation in helping them bring the brand purpose to vivid life.

Ralph Hamers
CEO and Chairman,
Executive Board, ING Group

Chairman, Management
Board Banking

Ralph Hamers was appointed a member of the Executive Board of ING Group—a Dutch multi-national banking and financial services corporation, and a Fortune Global 500 company—in 2013. He was then appointed CEO and Chairman of this Board shortly after. He joined ING in 1991. Prior to his appointment to the Executive Board, he was CEO of ING Belgium and Luxembourg.

Ralph Hamers is also Chairman of the Management Board Banking. He holds a Master of Science degree in Business Econometrics/Operations Research from Tilburg University in the Netherlands.

PART 1
WELCOME TO
THE FUTURE OF
YOUR BUSINESS

Ready or not, your business is being disrupted, impacting all aspects of your brand. A few innovations that challenge and inspire are:

15   5G: FIFTH-GENERATION
      WIRELESS STANDARD

17   AI/ML: ARTIFICIAL INTELLIGENCE
      AND MACHINE LEARNING

19   IOT: INTERNET OF THINGS

21   VR/AR/MR: VIRTUAL, AUGMENTED,
      AND MIXED REALITY

24   SUMMARY OF INNOVATIONS
      AND RELEVANCE FOR BRANDS

"We stand on the brink of a technological revolution that will fundamentally alter the way we live, work, and relate to one another. In its scale, scope, and complexity, the transformation will be unlike anything humankind has experienced before."

Klaus Schwab
Founder & Executive Chairman
World Economic Forum

The Fourth Industrial Revolution: What It Means and How Your Brand Responds

A caregiver places virtual reality (VR) gear over the head of an unresponsive nursing home patient. Within a few minutes, he is smiling and talking about being in paradise. The gear immerses him in realistic images and sounds. It looks and feels like he has been transported to a lush garden.

A woman shopping for furniture wants to make sure the pieces she likes will fit in her home. So she sets the furniture catalogue on the floor, scans it with a mobile phone app, and then sees how the pieces will look in her living room.

A model of electric cars has been found to overheat when charging. However, the owners don't have to bring their cars back to the dealership to be retrofitted; the cars get a software upgrade without leaving the garage—via Wi-Fi.

These are not scenes from a sci-fi movie. They're part of ordinary life as we write this book.

In Australia, health facilities are already using the Solis VR headsets to help trigger memories and positive emotions amongst persons with dementia. IKEA's augmented reality app and catalogue are already considered old news, having been released in 2013.

And by now, Tesla has wirelessly updated the Model S several times. The update in February 2017 enabled the car to parallel park autonomously.

In the retail space, the dawn of cashless, no-line, in-store purchases has arrived. One example is the recent prototype Amazon released in a video demo for its Amazon Go concept. The company describes it this way: "A mix of 'computer vision' along with 'deep learning algorithms' and 'sensor fusion' much like you'd find in self-driving cars." Their technology, dubbed "Just Walk Out," works by having you swipe a code on your mobile phone upon entry to the store. You then shop and walk out without standing in line or making a payment to a cashier. When you remove a product from a shelf or replace it, your movements are tracked with their virtual shopping cart. When you're done shopping, they send you a bill and receipt through your Amazon account.[1]

These are all manifestations of what the World Economic Forum refers to as the Fourth Industrial Revolution.[2]

"It is characterised by a fusion of technologies that is blurring the lines between the physical, digital, and biological spheres."

Klaus Schwab
Founder & Executive Chairman
World Economic Forum

The First Industrial Revolution came about with the use of water and steam power as well as mechanised production. Then electricity ushered in the Second Industrial Revolution, making mass production possible. The Third Industrial Revolution began when electronics and information technology automated production.

Finally, today's Fourth Industrial Revolution is the digital revolution, which is merging the physical, digital, and biological spheres, as noted in the statement by Klaus Schwab. This is a fast-developing trend, and we are considered to be in its early stages. It's what trend curator Rohit Bhargava calls an "accelerating present"—something that's already happening and will only accelerate in the near future.[3]

This technological revolution is changing just about all aspects of our lives, including how we care for the vulnerable and how we do business. For those of us charged with implementing and managing brand change, it will likely impact many aspects of the brand experiences we help to develop and deliver.

Disruptive Innovations in the Accelerating Present

We would like to highlight a few of the many technological developments with potential for even greater impact on our lives. You have likely heard of these developments, or may have already begun to integrate them in how your brand engages with customers and prospects. It could be that there are aspects helping your employees work more efficiently, whilst lessening tedious parts of their responsibilities.

Data privacy and security are already creating challenges

However, an important caution must be noted here. All of these developments are laden with immense privacy and security challenges for brands, around the exponential quantity of data and information with searchable specificity being gathered on a massive number of individuals. Data privacy and security are already creating challenges for organisations and could accelerate in the next few years.

One of the biggest challenges for brands in our digital age is how to put the right and most effective systems in place to navigate the landmines created around customer information gathering, use, and stewardship.

Although these technological developments have been topics of articles, videos, and presentations at industry conferences, their potential power and impact to your brand's future render them deserving of a review.

5G: FIFTH-GENERATION WIRELESS STANDARD

What It Is

You may be aware that your smartphone and other devices are running on 4G, or the fourth-generation mobile network. And they are running faster than ever. Well then, 5G, also known as fifth-generation mobile networks or fifth-generation wireless systems, is coming.

Aside from being fifty to one hundred times faster than 4G, 5G is expected to allow for a higher density of users, be more reliable, and have lower battery consumption. As such, this upgrade from 4G is not evolution-ary, says Simona Jankowski, senior research analyst at Goldman Sachs Research, but revolutionary.[4]

Although 5G is not expected to be fully available until 2020, companies are already preparing for it. AT&T announced it will launch 5G markets in Austin and Indianapolis (USA) this year, and they expect to provide theo-retical peak speeds of up to 1 Gbps.[5]

What It Means for Your Business

We will soon be living in a world powered by exponentially increasing amounts of data and high-speed connectivity. If you think information technology is fast now, 5G will put communications and data transfer on warp speed.

For brands, this will have huge implications in user experience and how you deliver your information, products, and services. Customers and prospects will expect all businesses and services to provide immediate responses, delivery, and problem resolution.

"It isn't just your connection speeds that are accelerating," says John Donovan, AT&T's chief strategy officer and group president, Technology and Operations, "but every element of the network becomes more seamless, efficient and capable".[6]

5G will greatly impact productivity and processes for employees

It's easy to conceive of how 5G will greatly impact productivity and processes for employees inside your organisation. Employers will be expected to do more when data transfer that used to take one hour can be completed in one minute, for example. Hopefully, those higher expectations will come with innovative ways to build and nurture employee trust and work-life balance.

AI/ML: ARTIFICIAL INTELLIGENCE AND MACHINE LEARNING

What It Is

Artificial intelligence (AI) refers to the ability of computers to "think" and behave intelligently. True AI, in which computers learn on their own, still only exists in fiction. In the movie *I, Robot*, for example, humanoid robots programmed to protect humans come to their own conclusion that they must rule over humans to save us from ourselves. That's not happening in real life...yet.

> We use machine learning every day when we look up a keyword on the Google search engine

We're getting closer to AI through machine learning (ML). Machine learning is when computers use pattern recognition to "learn" and respond accordingly. We use machine learning every day when we look up a keyword on the Google search engine. Google takes information from our past searching behaviour, our geographical location, and the actions of other users to understand what information we're looking for and to deliver websites that best meet our needs.

Another example of machine learning is Amazon's recommendation engine. It sees patterns in our product searches, previous purchases, and other customers' transactions to learn about our preferences and to suggest other products that are likely to be of interest.

What It Means for Your Business

As you may have realised, you're already using some form of emerging AI and machine learning in your daily life, including your work. If you haven't yet incorporated them into your business, you probably will. Very soon.

There are many implications in business. They include and extend beyond financial services reconciliation of funds to more personalised services in all kinds of industries, such as airline travel, healthcare, talent recruitment, retail, and more.

At the core of AI and related technologies is the desire to automate more mundane tasks in order to complete them faster. There is the ability to analyse a broader range of data—to deliver on more precise and specific customer demands. According to SAP Solutions,[7] machine learning can bring the following business benefits:

- Faster decision-making
- Adaptability
- Innovation and growth
- Unique insights
- Business acceleration
- Better outcomes

IOT: THE INTERNET OF THINGS

What It Is

The Internet of things (IoT) is the technological development wherein all sorts of devices are connected to the Internet. It's typical for our computers, smartphones, mobile devices, and printers to be connected. But that's not all.

Your home's thermostat and electric meter as well as your kitchen appliances, fitness tracker, and digital clocks may already be connected. In addition, cars, heart monitors, and washing machines could also be connected. We are told that anything with a sensor on it can be connected to the Internet. No wonder it has also been dubbed the Internet of Everything (IoE)—the intelligent connection of people, process, data, and things.[8]

According to Cisco Consulting Services, "The Internet of Everything (IoE) could generate $4.6 trillion in value for the global public sector by 2022 through cost savings, productivity gains, new revenues and improved citizen experiences."

> Anything with a sensor on it can be connected to the Internet

This is how Tesla can service its cars remotely through software updates. It's how you can turn on your home's furnace whilst you're still thirty minutes away, generating warmth by the time you arrive. And it's how Alexa in your Amazon Echo plays music from your iTunes account, answers your questions, reminds you of your appointments, and does so much more.

Experts predict that anywhere from 20 billion to 100 billion devices will be connected by 2020. That wide range in number of devices reflects the fact that the potential of IoT continues to develop.

What It Means for Your Business

"There are three major entities that will use IoT ecosystems: consumers, governments, and businesses," wrote Andrew Meola on Business Insider.[9] Some industries include manufacturing, transportation, defense, agriculture, infrastructure, retail, logistics, banking, oil, gas, mining, insurance, connected home, food services, utilities, hospitality, healthcare, smart buildings, and more. As you might have guessed from this long list, uses for IoT will continually emerge.

Each of these devices would be enabled to collect and transmit data, giving businesses super visibility. "Imagine utilities and telcos that can predict and prevent service outages, airlines that can remotely monitor and optimise plane performance, and healthcare organisations that can base treatment on real-time genome analysis. The business possibilities are endless," all examples SAP notes on their website.[10]

Smitha Rayala, product manager at SAP Leonardo, lists the business opportunities he believes IoT facilitates, summarised below:[11]

- **Optimise:** Gather data from connected devices and use them to optimise operations
- **Engage:** Engage customers by using the data to provide customised services
- **Integrate:** Use data within the enterprise ecosystem to enable real-time, dynamic decision-making
- **Innovate:** Use data about product usage to come up with new business models

VR/AR/MR: VIRTUAL, AUGMENTED, AND MIXED REALITY

What They Are

These adjacent technologies, which collectively have been called digital reality, provide different types of immersive experiences.

Virtual reality (VR) enables users to be immersed in a digital world they can explore by looking around and, in more advanced stages, by moving in the virtual space. This is what allows people who may be homebound, for example, to feel like they're standing in the middle of a beautiful garden.

> If you know of or have played Pokémon Go, then you know what this means

Augmented reality (AR) puts digital elements on top of your view of the real world. If you know of or have played Pokémon Go, then you know what this means. Your smartphone screen shows a Pokémon standing in front of you when in fact it isn't there; the AR feature of the game placed it there. This is also how IKEA's catalogue app makes it look like that sofa you're interested in is already in your living room.

Mixed reality (MR), as you may have guessed, combines VR and AR so that you see both the real environment and digital elements. The difference is that those virtual objects behave as if they were real. You can virtually rotate, lift, enlarge, move, and manipulate them in different ways.

What They Mean for Your Business

VR makes it possible to provide a multisensory experience, which leaves a lasting imprint on one's soul. If you're able to involve multiple senses at once, you imprint feelings on a person's hard disk. It's a much stronger and longer-lasting imprint compared to seeing a banner ad or TV advertisement, which involves only one or two senses at once. In other words, you convey the emotion around a brand and win over a person's heart for a long time. This is exactly the type of effective engagement that brand managers want to achieve.

With digital reality delivered by IoT and powered with 5G, almost any object can become a website, portal, or communication medium

Delivering this VR requires a smaller investment than creating a multisensory experience in a brick-and-mortar store. In fact, the in-person experience becomes unnecessary. Customers don't need to go to a showroom or a cinema for this interactive experience.

The sales cycle shortens as prospects enjoy the multisensory experience at home, in a café, or anywhere, for that matter. In the automotive industry, the dealership world will change as customers order and buy cars online. In architecture, people can explore the design of a new home before it has even been built.

All this significantly reduces our need for travel, whether for shopping or for working. When everyone has decent VR gear available, then face-to-face office meetings become less necessary. Employee training takes place virtually as well, without expensive and time-consuming travel.

AR, for its part, also allows brick-and-mortar retailers to take showroom experiences to the next level by blending digital and physical shopping. The virtual layer can provide a platform that allows improved communication, deeper engagement, and better personalisation.

As a result, brands deploying AR effectively will be able to provide differentiated interactions with physical products and customer experiences that seem richer than the ones provided by their online competitors.

Today, companies are already experimenting with AR and MR, trying to understand their audiences and grasp how their brands fit in this new environment. Companies must figure out what distinctive offerings they can produce and how to integrate them into omnichannel strategies.

These technologies are even more powerful when combined. With digital reality delivered by IoT and powered with 5G, almost any object can become a website, portal, or communication medium. "Users will start expecting brands to have mixed reality experiences in 2018," according to Robert Scoble. "The big money will show up in 2020."[12] It's all here now, and their integration by companies in many sectors is accelerating.

SUMMARY OF INNOVATIONS AND RELEVANCE FOR BRANDS

How the Fourth Industrial Revolution is Changing Everything

To summarise, here are just some of the ways the current industrial revolution is changing everything, availing opportunities as well as challenges for your brand:

Altered Buyer's Journey

"Seventy percent of the buying decision is made before a prospect talks to the company," says digital marketing expert Marcus Sheridan.[13] With so much information at their fingertips, customers rely less on sales staff to guide them on their purchasing decisions. And they want immediate answers on-demand.

Cutting-Edge Business Opportunities

We can't fully imagine the new business opportunities that will arise from the convergence of the physical and cyber worlds fueled by ultra-high-speed connectivity. Entrepreneurs with foresight are in the best position to identify and seize these opportunities.

Greater Data Collection

With an increasing number of devices connected to the Internet, huge amounts of data are being collected on all aspects of our daily lives. All this data can benefit businesses and customers alike. Businesses can increase production efficiency and offer hypercustomised solutions based on product use. At the same time, customers can use the data to save time, money, improve health, and so much more.

Bigger Security Concerns

Companies know which websites you've been surfing, how physically active you are, and even how much time per week you're spending on social media. The exponential proliferation of data and information gathering from connected devices has many implications about our security and privacy. All brands must become responsible stewards of the private information they gather and use. The minimum is abiding by the laws various organisations are scrambling to develop in an effort to keep up with the pace of technology. However, brands that go beyond those with customer data are likely to be favoured by customers.

Reinventing Marketing and Sales

Brands are learning how to extract insights from the data available to serve their customers better. For example, technology and utility consultant Seyi Fabode predicts that marketers will soon be able to deliver hyperlocally targeted ads, such as showing you a deal for the nearest grocery store as you're heading home.[14]

Diminishing Costs

Heath Terry, managing director at Goldman Sachs, predicts the increasing ability to pinpoint customer requirements will reduce logistics and inventory costs.[15] And as it gets easier for companies to deliver super-targeted solutions to customers, their ROI may increase.

New Staffing Requirements

Repetitive tasks are increasingly done by robots and computers, thereby freeing individuals to accomplish more and to focus on innovation and creativity. At ING Group, for example, the physical branch of retail banking has been replaced by the mobile phone in your pocket. Now you can complete several transactions with your smartphone that previously required in-person meetings with a professional.

Enhanced Productivity

Better connectivity and hyperspeed communication are changing how we collaborate and work. Already, many companies are hiring employees from different countries and across several time zones. An increasing number of freelancers, employees, and consultants are embracing digital nomadism, a lifestyle in which they can work from anywhere as long as they have a computer and Internet connection.

These are only some of the evolving implications of the Fourth Industrial Revolution for your brand and business. As you are probably now aware, it brings both opportunities and challenges, since your competitors could potentially access and integrate these developments as you might.

At the very least, they all require a mindset shift. It cannot be business as usual. In fact, you may have already begun to grapple with ways to either counteract or leverage some of these innovations for the benefit of your organisation and customers.

The good news is that if you are proactive in harnessing and integrating tools of our digitally dynamic age, you will have a head start in positioning for future competitive advantage. "Growth and the pace of technological change is leading to 'significant strategic shifts' as companies across industries re-evaluate their business strategies or consider consolidation in order to compete differently," says David Solomon, president and cochief operating officer of Goldman Sachs.[16]

The Challenge for Your Brand

Your brand, the enabler of your business, must transform to ensure your business thrives. You already know that your brand is much more than a marketing tool. Its effective implementation, ongoing management, monitoring, and evolution are critical.

You are also likely aware that social media has made this the age of the customer. Transparency is the new normal, since a comment or tweet can help or harm your brand—whether by a customer or even a current or past employee.

This drives the way your marketplace perceives and experiences all points of interaction with your organisation—as the sum of all your parts. According to Brand Finance, your brand represents 18 percent of your organisation's marketplace value.

As these and other developments of our Fourth Industrial Revolution require, constant change is the order of the day for the foreseeable future. Embracing these opportunities and addressing the challenges of our new age, are key. There are new ways to improve business across a range of industries, from small, regional companies to built environments, nonprofits, governmental and nongovernmental organisations.

What Do You Do in this Ocean of Change?

Get back to one of your most important business cores: your brand. Clarify your purpose. Hone in on the most essential offers that you can continue to refine. Keep learning about these fast-moving developments and look for ways to reestablish your unique ownership in focused areas.

For your brand, this is how we see the order of accountability: employees first; clients/customers second; and prospects, shareholders, and others third. Ask yourself how the Fourth Industrial Revolution will alter their experiences. How might your products and services be improved? Would your cost of doing business be reduced? Would your supply chain and productivity be positively affected?

Become familiar with these fast-moving developments of digital transformations. Begin to explore them if you haven't yet done so. By immersing yourself in these quickly evolving developments, you will spur your creativity and imagination of what can be done for and with your brand. Rest assured, if you don't do it, your competitors will.

Additional Learning

We have resources at our website (vim-group.com/futureproof) for further learning on the digital future and more. There you will find ways to access short videos, links, articles, and other content handpicked for time-strapped executives.

PART 2
BRAND PERFORMANCE STRATEGY FOR THE C-SUITE

33 BRAND VALUATION IN FOCUS

35 RETHINKING THE ROLE OF BRAND

41 QUICK STATS FOR THE BOARDROOM

43 COST OF A REBRAND

46 REASONS FOR BRAND CHANGE

50 LESSONS FROM MERGERS
AND ACQUISITIONS

52 HOW BRAND LICENSING AFFECTS
THE C-LEVEL DEBATE

54 THE NEW NORMAL OF
RETAIL EXPERIENCES

56 DELIVERING YOUR BRAND PROMISE

59 FROM NEW BRAND POSITIONING
TO IMPLEMENTATION

64 BRAND GOVERNANCE AND
MANAGEMENT ROI

68 INSIGHTS FOR FUTURE CHANGE

71 GETTING EMPLOYEES MORE INVOLVED

74 THE POWER OF A DIGITAL PLATFORM

77 FUTURE-PROOF BRAND BLUEPRINT

BRAND VALUATION IN FOCUS

Over the last thirteen years, we've been involved in sixty-plus brand valuation assignments commissioned by board members, finance, marketing, or communication directors. Their typical goals have been to obtain insight into the correlation between business performance, the brand, and organisational reputation.

Brands on the Balance Sheet

It has been a long journey to the financial world's increased recognition of brands. That recognition began with acquired brands only, with more comprehensive metrics that recognise in-house systems, forthcoming. Moreover, the CFO's awareness of the brand as the organisation's most valuable intangible asset continues to grow.

Establishing the Link Between Brand Value and Shareholder Value

This is supported by news from Brand Finance. They've announced that Solactive AG is setting up an index fund solely created to track the link between brand value and shareholder value. Also, according to a Brand Finance study, the average return between 2007 and 2015 across the S&P 500 was 49 percent. However, if Brand Finance's data was used to create index funds each year, investors could have generated returns of 97 percent.

Who Owns the Brand Equity Domain Internally Now?

Here there's no confusion. The brand still primarily remains with the marketing and/or branding groups. For marketers though, it's important

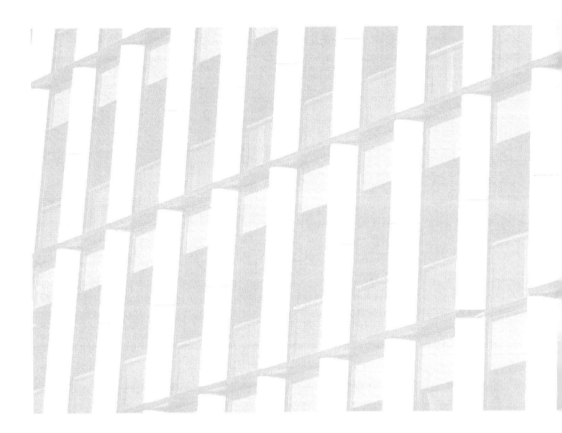

to understand how the financial domain is dealing with brand value, as this might affect decisions on branding as well. We see a lot of confusion around the term brand equity. For marketers, this is the set of drivers that attract customers and audiences by differentiating from other brands. For financial teams, equity refers to financial capital gained in a company, which is a totally different thing.

More interaction, discussion, and education are needed to bridge this understanding gap in the future. We believe that most of the driving has to be initiated by marketers, as they're typically steering brands. They also need to pave the way for more sophisticated brand management. In a world where the dialogue in boardrooms is mostly quantitative, the justification for all actions needs to be substantiated in this language.

RETHINKING THE ROLE OF BRAND

Brands must integrate the reality of the digital age into their design. Those who don't, or do so at a slower rate than others, will soon stand out as being old-fashioned and irrelevant. This integration is no longer an option, as the status quo is being disrupted in many industries.

As previously noted, there are a number of factors influencing the need for brands to continually evolve in our age of digital transformation. Beyond those technological breakthroughs outlined, social media has helped to make this the age of the customer. We've gathered some pertinent insights over the last two years on the impact of digital on design that we'd like to share. This list is far from complete. However, it contains insights and lessons from our recent work.

Very Limited Space

Imagine that a brand's space to express itself is limited to a small screen only. Design has become user-centric and much more visual. Incorporating infographics and icons helps with improved user experience (UX) and user interface (UI). Next, fonts are selected for easier reading online, and photography has completely different requirements than before. The practice of graphic design is fading away as a result. Design briefs have become more comprehensive, as we work to anticipate changes in the constantly evolving design landscape.

New Ecosystems are Emerging

We see digital and ad agencies entering the space of branding. Design agencies, coming in from the world of programmatic advertising, are building websites, or digital campaigns. Whilst digital services firms don't originally come from the design and strategic branding background, they manage to convince clients to work with them. They are seen to be more digital—whatever that may mean—than branding and design agencies.

There is a challenge for branding agencies that now need to explain their worth as well as their added value when it comes to digital. This implies a paradigm shift for them, which should have taken place yesterday!

Immaturity of the Market

For brand owners, life isn't getting easier. On one hand, they are looking to insource creativity more and more in order to increase agility. On the other hand, they are unsure of the maturity and real ability of all the new players in this domain and what value they may add.

> For brand owners, life isn't getting easier

Consistence versus Coherence

Consistency has been the buzz word in creating brands for decades. It was engrained into education and in many people's thinking. It's closely tied to static systems and rules, which have changed completely as well. Within digital space and channels, which have multisensory functions, we're seeing modular design that makes room for coherence over consistence.

Together they form building blocks and elements that help maintain the intent of the brand they represent. Building blocks online are more interactive and dynamic. Because they are connected to behaviour, i.e. what happens when you click, hover, and so forth, they are used in more functional ways. Some examples are navigation and conversion, compared to the building blocks used in offline environments. These more functional elements such as buttons and icons are less able to communicate a specific brand image.

All in all, these are not small evolutionary changes. Disruption is now an ongoing state for brands. We're already seeing this in the business models of start-ups. The point is that it has fully arrived in the design of brands, and it's a huge opportunity that both brands and designers should embrace.

With the rise of new digital channels and budget cuts in the marketing communications department, new steps in communications are necessary. But which steps? Optimising and improving marketing and communications processes are noted as high priorities.

Recognise Trends

If you look at the current market, a few trends are immediately noticeable. One is the rise of mobile data traffic because of the increasing use of smartphones. Relevant content as a strategic tool is more important than ever. Having the customer as your central focus has always been the mantra. But how? And which channels make up the customer journey these days?

Just as important, how do we ensure we are building trust and a fulfilling work environment that help retain and attract the best employee talent? How do we help to foster collaboration amongst employees?

If you list all the steps in the choice selection and buying process, these trends are also noticeable. Online shopping is more prevalent. The mixture of finding information online and buying in stores seems to be more common.

One Path: Customer Journey

By mapping all the possible steps in the customer journey, you are looking at things from a customer's viewpoint. This helps increase customer satisfaction and allows your unique brand promise to prove itself. When you think like a customer, you'll be better able to address his or her pain points.

The customer journey is not only influenced by marketing and communications, but by other factors that are more difficult to control. The role of a salesperson, the influence of social media, in-store communications, your environment, and opinions of friends and family all play important roles.

Branding is Being Turned Upside Down

Yes, that's what we think, and we think it's wonderful! This means change, and with change comes challenges, opportunities, and of course, some risks.

Let's consider the reasons branding is going through this transformation. Most branding professionals have recognised that there's no effective way to communicate a message to an external audience unless internal colleagues know, understand, and believe it first. Alignment is key, and inside equals outside. How you engage with customers reflects your internal organisation.

There has also been an explosion in the number of interaction channels and touchpoints, and the rise of digital brings its own challenges when it comes to maintaining control and consistent brand strategy. These days, it's about orchestrating, listening, and maintaining a dialogue. It's also about collaborating, adapting, and coherence, not about controlling through one-way communication.

Lastly, an increasing number of young businesses are hitting incumbents across all sectors with their disruptive business models, often facilitated by the vast digital possibilities available. For many businesses, their online and digital presence are fairly well-funded, independent, and highly dynamic. However, branding is often considered as an afterthought with no clear strategy or vision.

So what's the outcome when all these factors are combined?

First and foremost, it means that interactivity and agility become increasingly important. In our experience, this can mean fundamentally rethinking the organisational set-up of any branding function as existing structures are often less flexible. Next is knowing your purpose and what it means. And ensuring intense sharing of this knowledge through internal education programmes is vital.

Organisational dimensions of branding within businesses are fascinating. When talking with clients and working on ways to explore the future, the trend we see is that creativity and content are being brought in-house, allowing for organisations to increase their agility in the marketplace. We also see that corporations understand the need for enduring internal engagement programmes in collaboration with human resources functions.

A long-term approach here is key, as instilling purpose into an organisation is more likely to take four to seven years, and not one year alone. For agencies, this can also mean having to embrace new business models in order to cope with changing dynamics on the client side.

If we can make one prediction, it is that those who get this transition right will become the chief brand officers in their organisations. Those who won't embrace change and embark on the journey, face losing relevance, and ultimately, function.

The Other Path: Company Journey

Where the customer journey is the external path, the company journey is internal. This path indicates the processes that exist within the organisation, and it shows which steps are needed to connect with the customer journey. That sounds logical and simple. However, in practice, both paths do not connect with each other in many instances.

There are internal obstacles that are unfortunately visible externally in the customer journey. Usually, the gaps in the customer journey are quickly closed, but the gaps in the company journey tend to be forgotten and left open. What do you need to do to get this process back on track?

Time for a New Path

For a lot of companies and organisations, it is not easy to choose a new path. Where do you start?

For now, let's start with a suggestion: close the online marketing department. Digital communication now leads, and it cannot be seen as a separate channel with its own messages, target groups, and brand promises.

Multichannel marketing starts within the organisation. Stop thinking inside the box, and tear down the internal walls of the marketing communications department. Remember that the overall business goal is the focus, not the channel. Start by determining the message and then decide how you will deploy via available channels and resources.

Subsequently, map out the desired content and create this content independent of any channels. Then the channel managers should optimise the content specifically for their channel.

This bold move requires courage, persuasion, and shared enthusiasm within the organisation. Let the results be your compass. Without detours, you will reach your goal at a lower cost. You will have improved direct customer contact and obtain a higher level of effectiveness because of streamlined traffic along the paths.

QUICK STATS FOR THE BOARDROOM

Consider some stats relevant to your brand valuation, implementation, and building trust for your brand. They will impact decisions you make around your brand and we suggest you glean insights from them.

18%
The percentage of market capitalisation of the world's largest organisations is their brand value (Brand Finance 2017)

1:20
The ratio of the agency-to-implementation spend when rebranding (VIM Group ImpactValuator™ 2015)

€780
The average rebranding cost per employee over the last five years (VIM Group ImpactValuator 2015)

0.5%
The typical percentage of annual revenue that rebranding costs global companies (VIM Group ImpactValuator 2015)

7 yrs
The average number of years between major brand changes (VIM Group ImpactValuator 2017), we believe this time frame will continue to be shortened

What's the Value of Employee Trust?

In his 2017 Harvard Business Review article "The Neuroscience of Trust," Paul J. Zak notes some important stats we believe are tied to your brand, it's mission, culture, and how employees feel about your organisation. Successful organisations must attract and retain the best talent, and trust is a key part of that. Strong brands start from within and, according to Zak, employees at high-trust companies reveal the following statistics.

74%	**106%**	**50%**
Less stress	more energy at work	higher productivity
13%	**76%**	**29%**
fewer sick days	more engagement	more satisfaction with their lives

This image, depicting results of successful brand change efforts, is worth reviewing (The Brand Ticker, 2015), showing examples of increased brand value after rebranding:

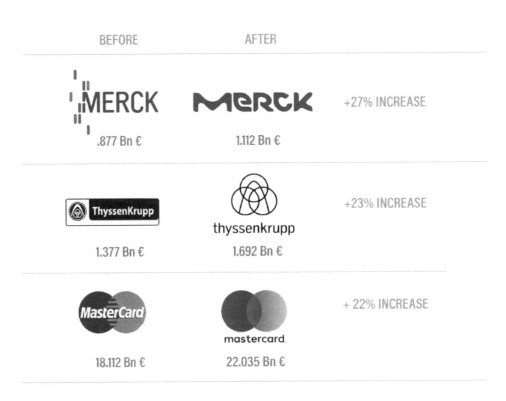

BEFORE	AFTER	
MERCK	MERCK	+27% INCREASE
.877 Bn €	1.112 Bn €	
ThyssenKrupp	thyssenkrupp	+23% INCREASE
1.377 Bn €	1.692 Bn €	
MasterCard	mastercard	+ 22% INCREASE
18.112 Bn €	22.035 Bn €	

COST OF A REBRAND

How Do You Even Begin to Put a Price Tag on a Rebrand?

So you're thinking about making a change to your brand. You have a new logo, perhaps some new design elements, or even a new name in mind, and you want to sell the idea to your key stakeholders. You have put together a strong visual proposal, and the new concept looks fantastic, but you know the first question on the minds of everyone in the room...How much is this going to cost, or save?

Cost Factors of Evolution versus Revolution

Let's consider some of the factors that can drive the brand change investment up or down.

The scope of your rebrand can have a huge impact on spending. Will it involve a simple logo swap or a full overhaul of your visual identity? The bigger the change, the deeper the consequences. Of course, it's not quite as simple as that, but it's a good rule of thumb.

Also take into consideration whether the new branding is an evolution of the existing brand components, or if it will completely revolutionise your look and feel. This impacts the way in which you implement, rollout, and manage your brand.

If your brand is to evolve, a rollout over time may suit the organisation, which can help reduce the spending by taking advantage of increased lead times and regular replacement cycles. However, a more revolutionary brand change would have greater impact on employees and customers alike if it is introduced via a "Big Bang" launch, immersing all stakeholders in the new brand from day one. Of course, this may be the costlier option. It is important to find the right balance of incremental spend versus impact.

There may be some important legal factors to take into consideration, as brand change can come with a hefty price tag. This is especially the case if your organisation sits within a highly regulated sector. For any organisation, a new logo or brand mark will need trademark protection, and any new externally designed fonts will need licensing. If the brand or company name is changing, there may also be further consequences when it comes to legal documentation or regulated labeling of products. Information on these will also need updating and processing through required approvals.

A Dedicated Project Team is Key

A rebrand can prove to be a complex project for any organisation. The best way to manage a project of this type is with a dedicated project team. Does

A dedicated project team is invaluable for a smooth rollout

your organisation have the necessary resources with the right skills in place to help carry the rebrand through to rollout and ongoing management? This can have implications on the overall budget for the project, as you may need to seek additional support. In our experience, we find that having a dedicated project team is invaluable for a smooth rollout and should be carefully considered when setting up the project organisation.

Planning, Priorities, and Phasing

When preparing for rollout, it can be helpful to consider any projects that might run concurrent with the rebrand that you can use as either a catalyst for the project or as a way to drive change through parts of the business.

It can also be helpful to consider when you will replace many of your items. If something is due to be changed in the very near future, you might apply a temporary solution for now and then use the regular replacement schedule for a thorough update.

We often see a conflict between ambition level and budgets with these types of projects. Sometimes the ambition far exceeds the constraints of the budget, and more realistic goals need to be set. In order to define a suitable budget for your project, it can be important to consider the business case for your initiative. Do you expect to have the support of the board and other key stakeholders, or do they need convincing? Do they see the financial benefits of building a stronger brand? Use financial data to demonstrate the value of the brand and to justify your rebrand spend. This can help convince those who set and approve budgets that it is in the organisation's best interest to make the appropriate investment.

Data-Driven Insights that Enable Action: ImpactValuator™

The main question of cost raises additional questions you should answer for your organisation because pricing a rebrand is not a quick or easy task. In fact, the question of cost is the one we get asked the most. Our ImpactValuator database, developed from data collected from clients since 2002, has been invaluable. It has helped us provide data-driven insights for navigating the pricing minefield, even before you start.

During our analyses of rebrand spend over the years, across our client-base, we've identified two key parameters which provide good indications for gauging the overall spend: revenue and headcount.

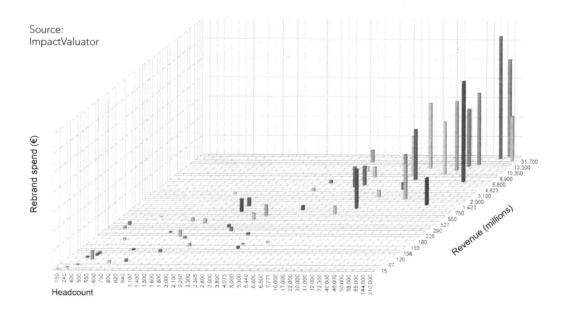

Source:
ImpactValuator

REASONS FOR BRAND CHANGE

Sooner or later the time comes when brand change becomes necessary. Recognising when this is the case may seem difficult. But in the life of a business, there are important markers that indicate when change is needed.

On average, organisations and brands change or update their brands about once every seven years. This often involves restyling logos, colour palettes, visual language, and the photographic style, in addition to strategic repositioning. In a small number of cases, the name of the organisation is also changed during this process. Although there is usually one leading reason for making the change, the motivation behind a rebranding project is often a combination of various factors. Here is an overview of the ten most common reasons for a corporate rebranding.

1. Mergers, Acquisitions, and Spin-offs

For the most part, changes in business ownership, such as mergers, acquisitions, and spin-offs, result in an immediate rebranding. The aim here is not only to make the change visible, but also to comply with legal and regulatory requirements. In the case of spin-offs—sometimes termed demergers—the newly created company is obliged to develop its own brand. This makes clear that it is no longer part of the larger organisation.

Over the past few years, this process has taken place at grid operators, which emerged from their energy companies. Some results have been the creation of companies such as Enexis, Alliander, and Stedin. There are several possibilities when it comes to mergers and acquisitions. The new company may develop a completely new brand, as in the case of @home, Casema, and Multikabel, which together became Ziggo. In other cases the name of one of the parties is used, e.g. Getronics, which continued under the KPN brand following its acquisition by KPN.

2. Repositioning

If implemented properly, a change to the positioning and brand promise of a company has major consequences for the organisation. Everything is adapted in line with the organisation's new strategy and promise, its products or services, HR policy, customer contact, corporate identity, and so on. Rebranding makes this change visible for all stakeholders. We saw an example of this with Gamma, which repositioned itself by moving away from traditional home improvements (DIY—do it yourself) and towards interiors and enjoyment.

3. Internationalisation

In some cases, rebranding is necessary so that a brand can also be used internationally. This may be because the brand name is too specific to a particular country. In certain countries, a brand name may also conjure up the wrong associations. Organisations that sell the same products in several countries, but under different brand names, are also increasingly opting to use one brand internationally. Famous examples include the rebranding of Jif to Cif, Smiths to Lay's, Raider to Twix, and Postbank (which was only used in the Netherlands) to ING, the brand that is used everywhere internationally.

4. Changing Markets

For some companies, changes in the marketplace mean that their very existence comes under threat. The digital transformation of society in particular is making it necessary for certain sectors to reinvent themselves. Different requirements call for a different product to be offered. One example in the Netherlands, the Free Record Shop, adapted its logo, corporate identity, and retail environment to give its brand a boost.

5. Bad Reputation

If a brand has a bad reputation and this is having a serious impact on its operating results, rebranding can ensure that negative associations with the brand are ameliorated or dispelled. It is important here that changes are implemented both internally and externally. This is the only way that a rebranding project can remove any negative associations with the brand and succeed. The rebranding of VendexKBB to Maxeda is one example of this.

6. Conflict with Stakeholders

Developing a brand may in itself also lead to a rebranding. This may be because the new style is too similar to an existing brand, for example. Such a situation was faced by Multimate, which, after its rebranding, lost a lawsuit against IKEA as the two brands had become too similar. Multimate had to make sure that its new logo was no longer visible within a period of six months.

Another reason is that aspects of a rebranding can sometimes be so negatively received by internal and external stakeholders that it stands in the way of the organisation's success. One example involved the identity change by Gap clothing company, which decided within one week that it would keep its original logo after all.

> A new CEO often brings a new lease on life to an organisation

7. New CEO

A new CEO often brings a new lease on life to an organisation. This may result in major organisational changes that also influence the course the company takes. Such a situation arose at Apple, for example, following the return of Steve Jobs in 1997. At that time Apple had to change in order to survive. Jobs himself took a hand in choosing the new logo, which changed from the rainbow-coloured apple to the more modern metallic variant, in addition to steering the company's shift in the modern era.

8. Outdated Image

One of the most common reasons for undertaking a corporate rebranding project is modernisation. Trends mean that over time brands come across as old-fashioned if they have not been updated. Although in many cases it is not the main reason, a more modern image is often one of the motivations behind a rebranding project.

9. Changing Brand Portfolio

Over the years, some organisations develop or acquire new brands. In time, this results in a broad brand portfolio that is no longer coherent. Furthermore, carrying many different brands often leads to high costs when it comes to maintaining and promoting the brand. In such cases, rebranding ensures that the entire brand portfolio is brought into line and tells a clear story about the organisation. A number of years ago, USG People rationalised and coordinated its brand portfolio in this way.

10. Further Development of Brand Components

Years ago, for the majority of organisations, a corporate identity consisted of just a logo, a primary colour palette, and typography. Brand elements such as photographic style, visual language, and a secondary colour palette had not been defined back then. This meant that there was a great deal of freedom when it came to applying the elements, with the result that the brand expressions ultimately became misaligned. In such cases, the further development of an organisation's brand is a must to ensure it is coherent and recognisable.

Since a new name can be part of brand change, here are the top four reasons for changing a company name:

Change of ownership	Change of business strategy	Change to competitive position	Change of business environment

LESSONS FROM MERGERS AND ACQUISITIONS

Market Value versus Brand Value

It is important to reflect on the role of brands during mergers and acquisitions and to consider the opportunities they provide. Unfortunately, it turns out that a great number of mergers fail in terms of market value. The resulting total value is often lower than the value of each individual part.

It is easy to say that this could have been prevented by paying more attention to the brand, but blind trust in market value is not a guarantee for success. It is a fact that, on average, 18 percent of the market capitalisation of the world's largest organisations is their brand value (Brand Finance 2017). This should be an incentive to immediately treat the brand as a strategic asset at the start of an acquisition. The merger between Ahold and Delhaize can be seen as a careful integration of two big and respected brands.

Even though Ahold had 61 percent of the shares, to the outside world it was presented to be a merger of equals. As a result, these two strong brands are not being pitted against each other. The acquisition was seen as reinforcing the brand perception of the stores of Albert Heijn and Delhaize, both in the domestic market in the Netherlands and Belgium as well as in the international growth markets.

> Brand awareness should be the warm blanket that covers the merger

There are also mergers that either don't work out as intended or have a bumpy start. For instance, the merger between Ziggo and UPC led to a lot of inconvenience and complaints from their customers. The road to an optimal brand experience of the new combined brands is long, and the question is whether this cable company can actually develop itself as a valuable brand.

Increased Investment in Brand Management

Often stakeholders do not adequately consider the brand during a merger or acquisition. This is a missed opportunity. The brand is a business enabler, a strategically important factor within mergers and acquisitions that has to have a key position in decisions. The brand is no longer a *thing* to be dealt with by the brand manager.

In many organisations it becomes clear that it is of actual financial value. The brand and brand management should be strategic starting points for all activities in a merger, not only with regard to external activities, but also for internal activities. Dedicated and motivated employees play a crucial role in the total valuation, which can be achieved by successfully unifying the two organisational cultures.

Brand in the War Room

What is the impact of a merger on a brand? What is the proposition of the combined products and services? These kinds of questions deserve focused attention from the board of directors and consultants when making important decisions about the planned merger or acquisition. These decisive factors should exceed a simple sum of parts and the combined shareholder value.

The ultimate added value can be found in the level of attention towards brand value. Brand managers should be invited into the war room, and they should demonstrate how the brand can be leveraged in a commercial and strategic way. In fact, brand awareness should be the warm blanket that covers the merger.

HOW BRAND LICENSING AFFECTS THE C-LEVEL DEBATE

This is one of our favourite topics with board members, specifically when it comes to licensing the corporate brand—or not. Ultimately, it doesn't truly matter whether a brand considers licensing; simply assessing your options gets you into a thorough discussion of the true value of branding and brand management. At the end of the day, your brand is your organisation's most important intellectual asset, and it deserves to be treated as such.

Too often, we notice that many marketing, brand, or communication directors don't fully understand the relationship between the value of the brand as an asset and the investment level it requires. CFOs do grasp the concept, and this is the time to initiate a discussion with their directors. CFOs should emphasise that the brand needs to be treated as a strategic investment like any other asset, and that investments need to be maintained over time, at a cost.

Exploring the Concept

Before we go into more detail on the subject of brand licensing, let's explore the concept further. The idea of licensing is that you give someone else (the licensee) the right to use your brand (you're the licensor) for a certain value, expressed as a percentage of turnover or revenue (the royalty).

The simplest example is that you can buy a white cap without a logo for €1.95. Whereas the same cap with a Nike swoosh stitched on it sells for €14.95. Hence, you can imagine that having the intellectual property rights to apply this swoosh has a value of somewhere between €0 and €13.95.

So, How Does it Work?

The licensee would never want to pay the whole difference, as he then wouldn't be able to generate any margin. Hence the exercise would become pointless.

In the business world, this implies that there's a market for how much royalty one would pay for brands. Obviously, the royalty will vary mostly based on two parameters:

- The sector: luxury goods will command a higher royalty than commodity goods
- The strength of a brand in a sector: strong brands—stronger then their peers—will command a higher royalty range

We will not elaborate further on exactly what it is that gets licensed in legal terms. For now we'll assume it's the trademark and associated rights that go with it.

The Relevance of Licensing for Corporate Brands

Similar to how licensing works for brands externally, many international organisations own the brand at a group level, or within a *Brandcompany* (a separate legal entity that owns the intellectual property rights of the corporate brand or organisation). This is done to protect the ownership of the brand where there are transactions within the business, and to ensure that the ownership is secured. In exchange, the Brandcompany charges an internal royalty fee to its operating companies.

Apart from the legal ownership and protection-perspective, this construct offers great opportunities for setting up a decent infrastructure and the governance for managing the brand across an organisation. The simple fact is that the operating companies pay a charge which comes with a license or royalty agreement, and within this agreement, the rights and obligations for its use are specified. With this agreement in place, the management of the brand is more strongly governed.

As you can imagine and might know from your own experience, there are many internal discussions about how to manage and use a brand within organisations. We recommend to always check the applicability of a potential Brandcompany construct with the internal tax department, as the international framework of tax rulings sometimes enables synergies in this area. Different to many strategic synergies and benefits, the tax synergies are cash-advantages for organisations when applicable after thorough analysis.

THE NEW NORMAL OF RETAIL EXPERIENCES

About a year ago, the rollout of the new KPN retail brand experience began. KPN is the largest telecom and IT services provider in the Netherlands, employing around eighteen thousand employees and operating more than one hundred stores.

The reason that we want to highlight this particular new retail brand experience is that it is revolutionary in both its user experience (UX) and customer experience (CX) and in its application of technology. This new concept is already paying off in dividends through higher revenue and improved connectivity between the online and offline experience.

The easiest way to describe why this is the new normal is as follows: instead of wall-to-wall shelves, cabinets, and POS (point-of-sale) materials, this store doesn't have any cabinets or shelves on the walls at all. The moment you walk in you begin asking yourself, "Hmmm, what's so different here?" This is when you see that all of the walls, with the exception of the glass entry, consist of floor-to-ceiling digital screens. The functionality of the screens varies. On some, you are able to touch the screens in order to configure a phone or contract, and others display branded videos and relevant content.

You may think, so what? We immediately start thinking about how this has come together from an organisational perspective. There are great possibilities to consider here.

Firstly, by plastering a retail environment with screens (smart walls), you almost eliminate the need for traditional shop-fitting. A different set of vendors are required in order to create an experience like this, which is bad news for the traditional shop-fitting industry.

Secondly, there's the need for continuous availability of relevant content. Due to the development of new technologies such as infrared, Kinect, touch, RFID, and more, the requirements for content are completely different from what they used to be in the old retail branding world.

> There's a need for retailers to radically reorganise internally in order to keep up

Thirdly, imagine the impact not only on vendors, but also on the organisation's internal set-up. Like many retailers, KPN used to be organised to accommodate supplier and vendor products and services. As this world is now changing radically, it means that there's a need for retailers to radically reorganise internally in order to keep up. Some functions are disappearing, and other functions with new requirements for different skill sets are being created in their place.

Lastly, the need for IT connectivity is different from what it used to be. It is no longer a matter of IT being used only for transactional functions and security. Now IT needs to ensure a seamless exchange of data and interactivity on the screens and the many functionalities that come with it. In order to ensure that the correct information is displayed in the right place at the right time, excellent internal coordination between marketing and IT is crucial, where previously they had never been this closely connected.

DELIVERING YOUR BRAND PROMISE

Strong brands make credible, relevant, and distinctive brand promises. Even more importantly, they fulfill these every day.

Developments in social media and other digital innovations have changed the world of brands. It has become a zillion-channel place where anyone can express his opinion about your brand and broadcast that opinion to many.

So how can you deal with this? The answer is simple: with trust. The execution, however, is far more complex.

People need to be able to trust your brand, and this includes your employees. Building trust requires a shift in those that steward brands within organisations. We have learnt that it is important to "Promise and Prove" on your core purpose at the same time.

Trust is the lever here. Your market has to trust your brand. Who would you trust more than your own family and friends who have just told you how amazing an experience was that they had at Starbucks, for instance? Within the multichannel world in which we live, an objective, positive message is easily spread. And a negative message probably spreads even more easily. So keep your brand promise in focus, and map how your brand delivers on it.

With this as our starting point, let's review our definition of a brand promise.

Brand Promise

The brand promise clarifies what the brand stands for, and it is one of the most important reasons for stakeholders to choose a particular brand. Often this promise is communicated explicitly through a slogan or tagline, but it can also be conveyed implicitly via communication with and behaviour towards stakeholders.

Brand success results from a relevant brand promise that is proven throughout the organisation. Every single day it is visible as the DNA of the organisation. This was addressed in 1997 by Steve Jobs: "To me, marketing is about values. This is a very complicated world; it's a very noisy world. And we're not going to get the chance to get people to remember much about us. No company is. So we have to be really clear on what we want them to know about us."

So what it boils down to is that for every moment your brand is in contact with stakeholders, you want to give them the correct look and feel of your brand. This means that you have to strive for coherence in your promise.

Brand Proof Points

The least a customer should expect from a brand is that the experience with the brand lives up to the promise made. The brand proof should at least be equal to the brand promise to avoid disappointing the customer. To prove the brand promise, everything has to be in place. Customers have to experience the brand promise through all the different channels: via the telephone, in all the stores/locations, on the website, other digital channels, and in face-to-face contact.

Social and technological developments now make it necessary to prove what you promise in your communication. Consumers are becoming more assertive and, with the launch of social media platforms like Twitter and Facebook, they are able to broadcast their opinions to many followers and friends. If a brand promise is not in harmony with the brand proof, this can be communicated in an instant to large groups of people located all over the world. The result is that the credibility of the brand is eroded.

For many years, a brand was supposed to have an attractive exterior. These days, the promise is regarded as the core driver of behaviour. The external focus of the brand—supported by attractive television commercials and eye-catching ad campaigns—has given way to seeing the brand as the guiding principle for the entire organisation. A brand touchpoint is any place (online and offline) a brand interacts with customers, employees, partners, and other stakeholders. When brand touchpoints demonstrate the brand promise, we refer to them as brand proof points.

One Example: Starbucks

A good example of a brand with a consistent brand promise and brand proof is Starbucks. Employees are friendly and quick, and the atmosphere is inviting with modern furniture, relaxed music, and pleasant aromas. Moreover, their range of products is the same all over the world. The company is likely to behave responsibly towards people and the environment. Most notably, they communicate their brand promise everywhere in exactly the same manner—not just in the stores, but also on Twitter, Facebook, the corporate website, everywhere. They are welcoming, provide a fast service, and it's clear they are passionate about coffee.

FROM NEW BRAND POSITIONING TO IMPLEMENTATION

A strong brand position is the foundation of a successful organisation. For example, how an organisation portrays itself to the market is most commonly determined by its brand personality, brand values and brand promise. These characteristics define how the brand will be perceived.

Brand changes require a significant amount of time. Time and energy are needed to come to a consensus about which characteristics of the organisation are most relevant; will fit the best; resonate with employees; and are the most distinctive compared to the competition.

After the brand positioning has been defined, it must be implemented across the organisation. This is a much harder task than the development of the positioning. Where do you start? Merely expressing your brand's positioning in your communication is no longer sufficient to gain trust from your marketplace, employees, and various audiences. A strong brand lives and breathes its positioning, not only in its marketing and communications, but in everything it does.

It is about the characteristics of all the products and services and the experience around the brand at every touchpoint, in every way. If you want to do this the right way, then it pays to get the whole organisation involved and not limit yourself to only involving the marketing communications, or brand management departments.

There are a number of steps that will help you to successfully implement your new brand position across your organisation.

The Preparation

A successful brand position implementation starts with smart planning and preparation. The positioning is an outline of what the brand stands for.

In most cases, it is still too complex and abstract to be immediately applied in all the parts of the organisation. Make the brand positioning concrete: what can customers expect from the brand at every brand touchpoint? To get prepared for the actual implementation, follow these five steps:

1. Determine the most important contact moments and/or channels

Start by determining which categories of contact moments or points are the most relevant for your organisation. Select a maximum of five. Unsure which channels to select? Find out what your moments of truth are in the customer journey by asking your customers about their experiences. Doing so should help you gather sufficient evidence to choose the best channels. For each of these channels you'll determine (Step 5) what the positioning will mean for the experience in that specific channel.

2. Summarise the brand positioning in concise promises

A good brand positioning consists of multiple elements. In most cases we see a brand personality and values, but we also regularly see elements like target groups, essence, promises and benefits. It is important that the positioning is translated into a few concise descriptions that represent the brand. Ideally, these are a focus on, or an explanation of, the central brand promise. Choose a maximum of four in order to be able to create an un-ambiguous view of your organisation.

3. Examine the gap between promise and proof

The next step is to determine the extent to which the recently formulated promises are being proven. Any gap between promises and proof needs to be examined and fixed. Start with collecting this information from internal stakeholders. Select a diverse group of stakeholders who can function as brand ambassadors at a later stage and who can also play an important role in carrying out and improving the brand positioning.

4. Map the needs and expectations of customers and prospects

With the input of these brand ambassadors, you'll have a good base to map the experiences, expectations and needs from your customers. How do customers experience the brand at the moment? Is this in line with your promises? And with these promises in mind, what do customers think the brand can bring them? What do they hope for? This information is valuable input to make the brand positioning more specific.

5. Determine the ways the positioning is brought to life at the most important contact moments

With your prior research of employees and customers, a large amount of information has already been gathered. Probably a bit too much. Give priority to the best ideas. Incorporate them into a guide for translating the positioning into concrete characteristics of the most important contact moments and/or channels of the organisation. With a group of deci-sion-making colleagues who are also involved with the most important contact moments (Step 1), you now can determine how each promise is proven in each channel by identifying global starting points. This can then be specified further in the actual implementation for your various departments and colleagues.

The Actual Implementation

The positioning affects everyone in the organisation, so we recommend implementing it in a cascading fashion: top-down from business units to departments to individual employees. Each department within the organi-sation writes down what the positioning means for their tasks and respon-sibilities and makes sure the changes are implemented. By letting your colleagues actually work with the positioning and by showing them what it means in their day-to-day activities, they will be understood and accepted within the whole organisation.

It is important to remain in control of this cascade, so that you keep the original idea intact. This is an important task for the brand manager and

people responsible for important customer contact moments who are involved from the first phase of the project. They should be available for questions, and to be involved in continued testing to ensure that the ideas generated are in line with the original goals.

Careful Monitoring and Continual Evaluation

The implementation is not a snapshot; it is a continuous process. That is why it is important to keep monitoring the brand performance. Is the brand positioning visible at all brand touchpoints? If that is not the case, why not?

> Internal acceptance of the new brand is one of the biggest challenges during a rebranding

By carefully monitoring the brand, small adjustments can be made to make the experience optimal for your customers and colleagues. This is how you develop a strong brand, as well as a successful organisation. It is also how you will be better prepared for more revolutionary brand change when the time comes.

Implementation and Activation

During this phase, the design and programmes developed are implemented at each of the brand proof points. This means that the new corporate brand is applied to all brand carriers and, in addition, the internal change programmes and external campaigns are launched. This might also mean that a new way of working is initiated.

The introduction of a new or revised brand often brings a lot of tension and uncertainty to an organisation. Employees are not always enthusiastic when a new brand is introduced. Internal acceptance of the new brand is one of the biggest challenges during a rebranding, as shown below.

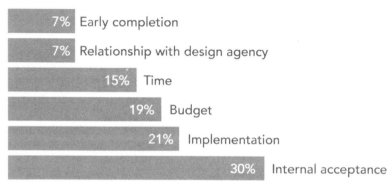

7%	Early completion
7%	Relationship with design agency
15%	Time
19%	Budget
21%	Implementation
30%	Internal acceptance

Source: Paulmann 2010

The greater the change, the larger the impact will be on internal resistance (Krokké, Bolhuis and Van Vuuren 2014).

Since this can have negative consequences for the way in which some employees react to the revised brand, it is important to pay attention to this part. Adequate communication before, during and after brand change is crucial to the success of the brand. This involves explaining how the change will be implemented and why the change is necessary.

This ought to be done by senior management. The commitment of your leadership is one of the most important pre-conditions. Visible support for the rebranding by senior management highlights the necessity for the change, and employees will be more inclined to cooperate. After this step has been taken, it is important to get the most important stakeholders enthusiastic about the new brand. A pre-established communication plan is essential to achieve this very important goal of full buy-in and cooperation by employees (Bolhuis, Van den Bosch, De Jonge, and Heuvelman 2014).

BRAND GOVERNANCE AND MANAGEMENT ROI

For most organisations, brand management starts with formulating a relevant, distinctive, and authentic brand promise. Often it is an intensive and lengthy project, making its delivery to the organisation already a victory. Yet, after a campaign to get the brand promise in the minds of internal and external stakeholders, active brand management stops in most organisations. Our Brand Life Cycle Model provides a structure for brand management over the long term.

Time to Start Using Brand Management

The discipline of brand management is still relatively new and broad. Because the brand should play a role in every layer of an organisation, the role of the brand manager can be enormously complex. There are no textbooks (yet), and there are only a handful of organisations that incorporate brand management. So the question is: How and where in the organisation do you begin forming a structure for brand management?

Identify and Evaluate the Condition of the Brand

Begin with an analysis amongst internal and external stakeholders: What are their perceptions of the brand? To what extent are these perceptions consistent with the brand promise? And more importantly, which brand experiences have influenced their feelings and opinions?

Then categorise the brand touchpoints: what are the experiences with the product or service or communication with employees of the brand. This forms the basis for how the brand is perceived, both by staff and by potential customers. Next, analyse your highest priority touchpoints: to what extent do they deliver the brand promise? And to what extent do they jointly contribute to a consistent brand experience?

Create an Internal Brand Organisation Chart

Connect the findings mentioned above to the internal organisation: How do they contribute to a consistent and fitting brand experience? With the brand management—based on the Brand Life Cycle Model—you can structure your analysis by making distinctions between the internal Brand Organisation and the Brand Evaluation, Brand Strategy, Brand Development, Brand Implementation, and Brand Operations.

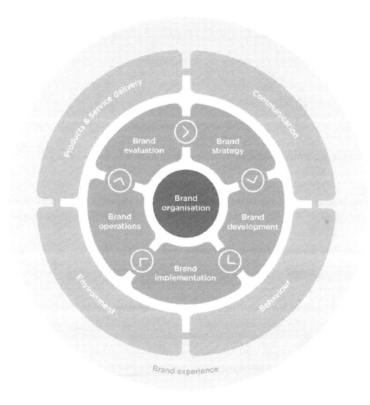

BRAND LIFE CYCLE MODEL

Brand Organisation

Define who should play a direct and indirect role in developing, managing, and implementing the brand and at what levels in the organisation these roles are placed. Measure how well the organisation is oriented around the brand, and use the brand as a starting point for action.

Brand Evaluation

Consider whether the brand attributes, e.g. persona, reputation, customer satisfaction, and employee engagement, are included in regular research. More importantly, what is done with this information? Also look at how well the brand is legally protected and how abuse of the brand is prevented.

Brand Strategy

Map out if the brand promise is still relevant, authentic, and distinctive. Check also to see if it is developed enough to serve as a basis for the development of products and/or services, for managing employees, and for creating communication.

Brand Development

The brand promise is made viable and visible by establishing principles for symbolism (corporate identity), communications (content), and behaviour that inform products and service delivery. These principles form the basis for all brand touchpoints.

The brand serves as a starting point for the entire organisation

Therefore, it is important to check whether these basic building blocks of the brand are fully developed and still represent the brand promise.

Brand Implementation

Clearly define which departments influence which brand touchpoints. Determine as to what extent the brand is included in processes that contribute to these brand touchpoints, and are there a sufficient amount of tools to facilitate a change? In addition, do not forget to evaluate the policies around essential customer processes. For example, how are complaint procedures in sync with the brand promise?

Brand Operations

The organisational structure and culture are the building blocks for the brand operations. There are approaches to operating the brand, ranging from engaging, collaborative, and proactive management to more rigid mandates and compliance. The pervasive style and dominant influences of the internal culture fundamentally impact the best governance tactics and practices for that particular organisation.

Let the Brand Promise Do its Job

By connecting cause (brand management) and effect (manifestation of the brand and brand perception), the basis for a structured roadmap is created with short- and long-term improvements for a more professional brand governance and management. The brand is not only the basis for communication and campaigns, but also serves as a starting point for the entire organisation. This is the best way to prove internally and externally what the brand promises.

INSIGHTS FOR FUTURE CHANGE

Too often, we have to talk with brand owners about where brand ownership sits, or should sit, internally. Usually the discussion will be about whether it's the chief communications officer, the chief marketing officer, or the new chief brand officer who should own brand management in the business.

The decision of where brand or brand management sits is dependent on many factors. By approaching the topic more holistically, we see the following considerations:

Brand architecture: Is the organisation mono-branded, endorsed, or product branded? Please see the review of brand architecture on the facing page.

Definition of What Brand Management Encompasses:

- Does internal branding sit within the brand function or within the communications or HR departments? In the case of mono-branding, is your above-the-line communication or mass-communication part of the function, or is that placed somewhere else—marketing for example?
- To what extent is digitalisation part of the remit, or does it sit within another corporate function?
- To what extent are content creation and design part of the remit?
- What is the philosophy or governance in terms of creating more agility? In a world where speed of adaptation and brand strategy come together, there's an argument to go for an in-house agency model, which then requires a heavier and more extensive corporate brand management function.

Brand Architecture

Let's review the three typical forms of brand architecture. Mono-branded is when there is one brand noted for all products and services of the corporate brand. The Nike organisation is an example of a mono-brand since the public typically sees the name Nike listed first, in front of its products and services. As a result, you have Nike Air, Nike Golf, Nike Stores, and more.

Amazon has examples of endorsed brands. You might see notations like: Alexa, an Amazon Company. Companies often integrate mono-branded and endorsed concepts. Amazon, in another instance, also positions its web services as AWS or Amazon Web Services.

The product-branded concept is often represented by umbrella companies of consumer products. Procter & Gamble is an example of an umbrella company with many products that customers often know by the specific products' brand name, and not that of Procter & Gamble. We may purchase Olay, or Tide, or Pampers without necessarily associating these products with Procter & Gamble.

No doubt you have come across companies that use all three types of brand architecture, which can result in confusion for customers.

With the three forms of brand architecture noted above, the more mono-branded, the more mature the corporate brand management function needs to be. This means the internal team has to have effective, centralised systems and experience in place to manage the brand most effectively.

Let's look a bit deeper at the digital effect.

With the impact of digital innovation on design, many brands will have to update their design as a consequence of digitalisation. Even if there isn't a brand update required from a positioning perspective, change is required to remain current and to avoid looking/feeling prematurely outdated.

Traditionally we've seen misalignment between IT and marketing and communications. Yet, with big data coming at us and digitalisation everywhere, it's a no-brainer that things will change. The challenge with big data is that it is hard to know what approach to take as it can seem all-encompassing and overwhelming. As we learnt long ago, it's best to take one step at a time. This is where marketing has an important role to play, to identify and prioritise opportunities on how to work with data. Here we see two dimensions:

- From an outside-in perspective—understanding audience behaviour, brand equity, and conversion
- The usage of market segmentation skills to discover what works and what doesn't

In our opinion, marketers should first analyse what works and what doesn't. Their adage should be to start small and test, then adapt and test again—until they've discovered what works well. Only then would it be wise to ramp up to bigger initiatives, where IT can play a more dominant role.

As for the future of brand management, we envision that it will remain a marketing or communications responsibility through engagement, exchange, and education. However, an understanding of IT is a must for every marketer to be successful in the next decade.

GETTING EMPLOYEES MORE INVOLVED

Traditionally, brand and marketing stewards are focused on the needs of customers, and for the most part, this still holds true. Equipped with the latest technology and strategies, brands try to delight customers with relevant products and services in order to give them the most appealing brand experiences. Large brands are increasingly building subtle bridges between suppliers and customers as services and products become increasingly smarter and more aligned with personal preferences. But what about the brand experience and involvement of employees? What is being done to involve employees just as much as customers?

Improving Brand Awareness

You've probably seen them, the tattle stickers on the back of a bus, truck, or pizza delivery vehicles. Stickers that are there to pressure employees into behaving a certain way in traffic and to be brand ambassadors. Is there no alternative? Those stickers would not be necessary if employees were involved with the brand in a more engaging way. It is time marketing also focused on the employees.

This is not the first time that someone has advocated for internal involvement, but often it remains just an idea or ad hoc initiative. Unfortunately, these situations hardly ever lead to lasting and positive brand awareness with employees. It is time to make brand awareness with employees a structural component of organisational success.

Brand management is a hot item within large organisations and goes beyond the brand manager. More often than not, it is becoming clear in boardrooms that the brand contributes to the business performance. Brands are increasingly strategic starting points for all activities. Companies that want to manage their brands properly will have to look beyond the classical marketing goals like sales, brand awareness, and product development. Modern brand management also takes the development and maintenance of internal brand involvement into account within the strategic goals. Only then will internal and external brand awareness improve.

Marketing and HR are in This Together

A brand is built from the inside to perform on the outside. Involved and motivated employees play a crucial role in the total value. This seems like an obvious truth, but why is the old adage "start from the inside to win on the outside" still implemented so poorly? Perhaps because the internal translation of the larger idea hasn't been done properly.

Often that is because marketing staff and HR professionals cannot communicate properly beyond their own focus. It is time for marketing staff and HR professionals to work together with other business units within the organisation and to commit themselves to sharing the responsibility of brand ownership. For instance, this could be done by structurally coordinating the marketing actions with the HR programme.

What if marketing considers all employees to be an internal target group? What would be their trigger? You could think of job applicants as a target group. Brand management starts when you walk in the door, and all target groups have to be considered when defining the marketing goals and subsequent communication.

> What if marketing considers all employees to be an internal target group?

Tips for Marketing and HR to Activate the Brand Experience Internally:

* Have a brand party for a new employee on his or her first day. HR is the appropriate department to create internal involvement alongside internal responsibility. This can help make employees aware that they play an important role in strengthening and improving the overall brand experience.

- Add brand responsibilities to job role descriptions and evaluations, letting employees know that they influence the brand experience and that it plays a role in their everyday tasks.

- Make internal involvement part of the marketing plan and consider employees as a target group.

- Make internal involvement measurable by making brand experience part of the research into employee involvement. In many companies, this research is already conducted on a regular basis, but employees are rarely asked how they experience the brand and what role the brand plays in their interaction with customers.

By creating an internal campaign together, marketing and HR can increase the internal brand experience. This will mean that tattle stickers are not necessary anymore, and internal involvement becomes a logical part of brand management, helping to drive brand value.

THE POWER OF A DIGITAL PLATFORM

The job is done, and the brand team and board are happy. The rebranding has been successfully completed, and the brand is launched. It is conceivable that on this festive milestone, brand coherence is in focus. This is precisely the ideal moment to start managing the brand.

A few weeks after the introduction of the new visual identity you start to see it happening. The PDF with the brand guidelines will be circulated, and both internal and external parties will enthusiastically get to work with the source files. Gone is the overview, the control you thought you had, as your precious brand disperses before your eyes.

The Brand Portal Contributes to a Stronger Brand

The brand strategy is fully integrated into the organisation when the brand portal is anchored into the core processes. As a direct result, the touch-points will always be on-brand—saving time and money for colleagues who use the brand elements and assets. In short, a well-executed brand portal contributes to a stronger brand.

Distributing Instead of Dispersing

We recommend you begin managing your brand by selecting a brand portal when you are getting prepared for your rebrand. It's better for your brand, and the brand manager needs this essential tool. A brand portal is much more than an online corporate identity manual. It is an online platform to optimally inform, facilitate, and inspire the internal and external users of the brand. By developing a brand portal, you avoid fragmentation, and you can maintain, increase, and prolong the interest that is there for the brand.

Brand Portals Come in All Shapes and Sizes

In a brand portal, all current corporate identity, brand guidelines, source files, brand building blocks, and designs of brand carriers come together. This occurs visually and textually, complete with examples and background information on the subject. Tools in a brand portal help make your work easier. For example, you can automatically format business cards or posters in accordance with the guidelines. An active brand portal functions as a community where brand users share and inspire one another. Through an automated approval process, the brand manager can see if everything is working according to the guidelines to ensure the right brand experience is being provided.

Content Strategy is Essential

You should formulate a content strategy for the brand portal, in which you determine how this great range of information can be transmitted in the best possible manner. Please pay attention to the type of visitor, learning behaviour of people, and the type of information you want to convey. A designer from an external agency

> An active brand portal functions as a community where brand users share

can probably use the specifications of an ad, but a marketing manager who then has to evaluate the branded item on the correct use of the brand style, cannot. The various target groups should be able to understand and apply the information.

There is a difference between need-to-know and nice-to-know information. Need-to-know information is essential information that should be readily available to all users, and the nice-to-know information may be more tucked away. For example, specifications and source files are useful for designers, but not relevant for everyone. This example could be given a permanent place in a submenu so that the designers find it quickly.

In short, make for an inviting navigation. For example, your goal should be that every visitor will be able to find what he or she needs within three clicks. The search function on a brand portal is an immense advantage over a static corporate identity manual in PDF.

Plea for an Open Door

Prevention is better than dispersing—that is the message of this plea. It seems obvious, but often the added value of a brand portal is underestimated, and a PDF as a corporate identity manual may seem to be sufficient. However, the portal is the means to improve the consistency, familiarity, coherence, and visual look of your brand.

A brand portal usually requires a higher investment than a corporate identity manual in PDF format. You have the ability to share guidelines with different audiences easily. Then you won't lose time in spreading the visual identity manual and source files, and you'll have control over versioning of guidelines and source files. In other words, the efficiency quickly delivers unparalleled savings in time and money. All of these factors greatly contribute to your brand getting stronger over the long run.

Our Digital Enablers section includes additional information on tools you'll need to plan, implement, and manage your brand.

FUTURE-PROOF BRAND BLUEPRINT

Depending on the reasons and goals for your brand change, there is a range of products and services that can help you achieve success and be better prepared for future change. We have mapped the key items in this visual blueprint, tied to our premise for this book, and what we believe is essential for ROI. Our proprietary processes and methodologies are outlined in greater detail in the next section. This visual blueprint depicts an overview of components we incorporate.

ImpactValuator (Cost Estimates and Industry Benchmarks)	ImpactValuator (Detailed, Customised Cost Estimates and Industry Benchmarks)	Initial Brand Performance Scan (w/ research and The Brand Ticker and Industry Benchmarks)	Rebrand Scenarios on Phasing and Investment Efficiencies
Data-Driven Insights + Predictive Analytics	Data-Driven Insights + Predictive Analytics	Data-Driven Insights + Predictive Analytics	Data-Driven Insights
Agency RFPs and Vendor Selection Guidance	Work Team Structure and Management	Transition Strategies and Value Engineering	Implementation Planning + Strategy
Logistics + Supply Chain Management	Logistics + Supply Chain Management	Logistics + Supply Chain Management	Logistics + Supply Chain Management
Execution Management: Procurement, Installation, Removals	Digital Asset Management Tools Review and Recommendations + Brand2Manage	Employee Engagement and Training	Brand Experience Interaction App
Logistics + Supply Chain Management	Logistics and Technology	Logistics and Technology	Logistics and Technology
Rollout Planning and Execution	Brand Governance and Management Structure	Brand Performance Valuator + Audit (Assessments w/ The Brand Ticker and Industry Benchmarks)	Ongoing Brand Monitoring and Insights for Future Change (Touchpoint + Digital Evolution)
Logistics + Supply Chain Management	Logistics + Supply Chain Management	Data-Driven Insights + Predictive Analytics	Data-Driven Insights + Predictive Analytics

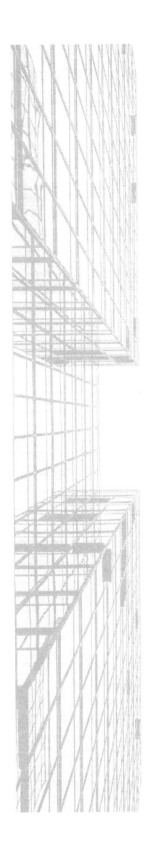

PART 3
BRAND CHANGE
AND MANAGEMENT
THAT DRIVES ROI

83 BRAND PERFORMANCE
    IMPROVEMENT PROCESS

92 BRAND CHANGE DELIVERY PROCESS

110 AN OVERVIEW OF DIGITAL ENABLERS
    AND MANAGEMENT TOOLS

In this part of the book we share our experience on
how to improve brand performance and how to drive
the brand change process. We also provide you with
an overview of digital enablers and management tools
we believe should be part of your toolkit for planning,
implementing, and managing your brand as you evolve.

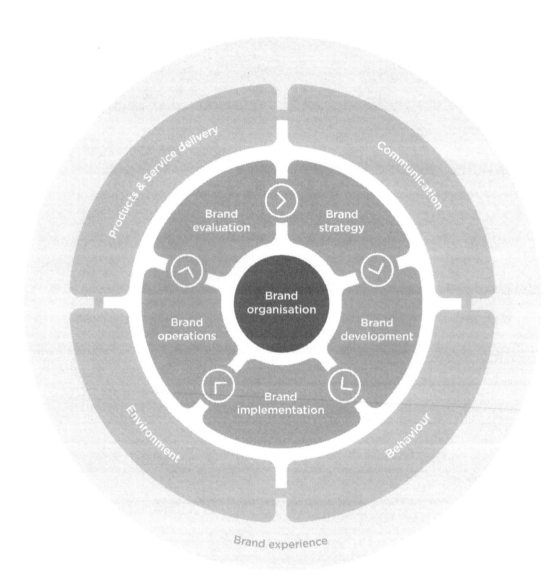

BRAND LIFE CYCLE MODEL

BRAND PERFORMANCE
IMPROVEMENT PROCESS

A brand is much more than a name or logo—a concept we've emphasised throughout this book. It consists of all forms of expression of an organisation by which target groups create an image of and feelings about your products, services, and organisation. Research resulting in the brand orientation index, by Johan Gromark, shows that organisations perform significantly better when they have a strong organised brand; hence a coherent brand experience at all brand touchpoints.

As previously stated, brand management is no longer the *thing* of the brand manager. It is becoming clear in boardrooms that the brand contributes to the business performance. Although brand performance is influenced by many factors, it starts within the organisation itself.

We believe that improving the quality and output of a company's internal branding organisation is the first and most important step to improving brand experience and performance. Based on how we have seen brand management operate within many large and internationally operating companies, we developed processes and tools to support

> It is becoming clear in boardrooms that the brand contributes to the business performance

you in delivering improved brand performance. Our Brand Life Cycle Model illustrates that the Brand Organisation sits at the core, surrounded by the five essential components for improved brand performance: Brand Evaluation, Brand Strategy, Brand Development, Brand Implementation, and Brand Operations.

This graphic shows examples of client-services per component or step of the Brand Life Cycle Model:

EVALUATION	STRATEGY	DEVELOPMENT	IMPLEMENTATION	OPERATIONS
Brand Research	Brand Business Strategy/Brand Project Plan	Design & Naming Architecture	Brand Implementation Management	Brand Operational Support
Preparation Research	Brand Positioning & Architecture	Brand Styling & Naming	Brand Activation	Brand Management Optimisation
	Brand Concept & Story	Brand Guidelines		Brand Analytics
		Brand Registration		

Brand Governance Structure for Brand Improvement

Before starting any brand improvement programme, it is crucial to establish the organisational structure and the brand governance structure. The topics that need to be explored are:

- Organisational preconditions to develop a project structure and a future brand governance model
- Ownership / senior management commitment
- Organisational structure, i.e. centralised vs decentralised
- Roles and responsibilities throughout the global organisation
- Capabilities and sourcing
- Available or necessary tooling
- Budget allocation
- Organisational culture and politics

Now that we have depicted the five components of our Brand Life Cycle Model, here is our five-step approach for Brand Improvement:

Our Overarching Approach for Brand Improvement

STEP 0: ASSESS STATUS QUO

Investigate and analyse the current and the desired situation

STEP 1: DEFINE IMPROVEMENT AREAS

Define the short-, middle-, and long-term improvements

STEP 2: CREATE ROADMAP

Create a roadmap and set the brand governance organisation for activation of the short-, middle-, and long-term improvements

STEP 3: ACTIVATE ROADMAP

Execute on the roadmap or realisation of the roadmap

STEP 4: MONITOR BY KPIs

Set a KPI (Key Performance Indicator) structure and create a relevant brand performance dashboard

STEP 0: ASSESS STATUS QUO

In order to make informed decisions on improving your brand performance, we developed the Brand Performance Scan. The Brand Performance Scan provides data-driven insights of the current state of brand
management, brand manifestation, and quality of the brand performance.

The Brand Performance Scan is based on the Brand Life Cycle Model.

We assess to what extent and through which brand touchpoints the brand
delivers on its promise. We then identify which internal factors influence
the brand performance. During this step, quantitative and qualitative data
will be collected via desk research, online questionnaires will be administered and stakeholder interviews are conducted.

BRAND LIFE CYCLE MODEL

BRAND MANAGEMENT

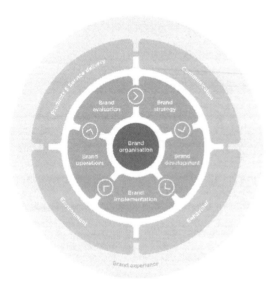

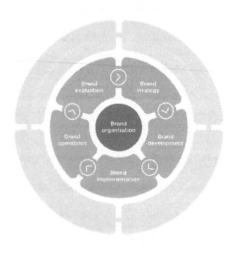

Measurement:

Maturity of brand management
organisation related to brand
documentation, processes, tools,
systems, and instruments

The data reveals information such as:

- Role of the brand within the organisation
- Current brand governance organisation
- Processes and assets
- Available tools (KPIs, guidelines, and brand management systems)
- Budgets and total cost of ownership

With the tooling to carry out the audit, improvements are localised and translated into actionable initiatives. In our view, the most important reason to translate the findings of the scan is a comprehensive roadmap for brand improvement. By means of a dashboard, both the current situation and changes since the previous measurements are reported.

BRAND MANIFESTATION

BRAND PERFORMANCE

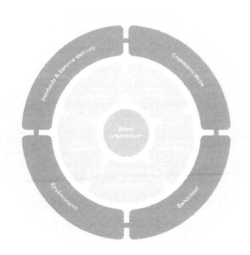

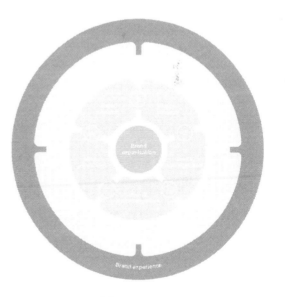

Measurement:

Consistency, coherency, quality, and fit of brand promise with the visual and verbal messages at select brand touchpoints

Measurement:

Brand experience per target audience: awareness, associations, attitude, and behaviour

STEP 1: DEFINE IMPROVEMENT AREAS

In this step, areas to be improved will be defined and discussed with the relevant stakeholders. The improvements are categorised as strategic, tactical, and operational, including the impact on people, processes, budget, and tooling. This step enables the organisation to take the right decisions and run the program. The short-, middle-, and long-term activities will be translated into an actionable roadmap:

- **Strategic level - long-term improvements**
  The long-term improvements provide insight into brand performance for stakeholders to raise the level of brand orientation within the company.

- **Tactical level - middle- to long-term improvements**
  The middle- to long-term improvements are initiatives developed to improve the quality of brand management and the organisation around the brand.

- **Operational level – short- to middle-term improvements**
  The short- to middle-term improvements provide insight into the quality of brand manifestation and lead to initiatives to improve brand implementation.

WORKSTREAMS

STRATEGIC THEMES			BRAND PROGRAMME MANAGEMENT
Align the Brand	Brand Portfolio & Architecture	Brand Positioning	
Facilitate and Guide Brand Implementation	Brand Governance	Brand Portal	
Measure the Brand	Brand Performance Measurement		
Bring the Brand to Life	Brand Experience		

STEP 2: CREATE ROADMAP

In this step, all initiatives will be ordered by priority in a roadmap—considering the dependencies with other running projects—and set within a timeline. This one- to three-year approach will ensure the longer term value creation, and it requires C-level approval for the right mandate. Within the brand governance structure, the different workstreams will be responsible for the detailed planning and activation.

Roles, responsibilities, and activities to be defined will include:

- Creating and establishing the internal workstream teams, e.g. marketing, facilities, communications, and digital
- Establishing and/or refining acceptance, change/deviation, risk, and escalation procedures
- Establishing the working parameters of the key brand advisory member of the team who will work closely with the Project Sponsor
- Agreeing on and setting up the consultation and reporting schedule

Below is an example of how the timeline of a complex improvement program might be mapped.

	PHASE 1			PHASE 2				PHASE 3			
	MAR	APR	MAY	JUN	JUL	AUG	SEP	OCT	NOV	DEC	Q1/Q2 '18
PROGRAM MNGT	Brand mngt plan / BL meeting	BL working sessions	VSP slide deck	Continuous program management							
PORTF. & ARCHITECT.	Draft portfolio	Finalise brand portfolio & architecture		Design architecture + M&A guide				Brand portfolio alignment			
POSITIONING	Positioning approach		Update positioning (alignment C-suite): briefing, agency selection, positioning			Design briefing & agency selection	Update brand style & messaging (incl. guidelines)	Develop specific guidelines, e.g. co-branding/sponsoring, tradeshows			
GOVERNANCE	Partner (3rd parties) listing and review	Define governance structure	Implement brand governance structure								
PORTAL		Brand portal audit	Brand portal strategy	Improve current/implement new brand portal & KPI dashboard integration							
PERF. MEASUREMENT	KPI shortlist	KPI framework, dashboard concept & measurement plan		Implementation of continuous brand performance measurement structure							
EXPERIENCE				Develop brand audit plan		Execute brand audit plan					
			Campaign requirements		Campaign briefing	Agency selection	Global brand campaign development				Global brand campaign execution

STEP 3: ACTIVATE ROADMAP

The focus in this step is to implement the roadmap.

Critical success factors are:

- C-level mandate and involvement
- A culture and organisational proof execution approach (centralised versus decentralised)
- Communication of results to all stakeholders
- Setting KPIs and monitoring over time

STEP 4: MONITOR BY KPIs

To ensure a longer-term improvement, monitoring your brand with the relevant KPI-setting is crucial. There are many brand measurement systems, and new online tools continually emerge. Too much data is available.

The real question is: what insights can you gain from these KPIs? Is the data relevant to your organisation? And more importantly, what can you do to improve and add value to the business goals?

The model below provides an overview of available systems and which questions they answer. We have outlined a breakdown by category (Marketing KPIs, Brand KPIs and Performance KPIs). Our Brand Performance Scan in Step 0 sources the relevant data from existing systems.

MARKETING KPIs	BRAND KPIs	PERFORMANCE KPIs
How effective and efficient are your marketing activities?	How well known and well regarded is your brand?	How much impact does your brand have on performance
- Targeting the right people - Sending the right message - Using the right media - Triggering the right response	- Brand awareness & familiarity - Brand presence (online) - Brand engagement & advocacy (NPS*) - Brand perceptions - Brand preference & loyalty - Brand reputation - Brand equity/ valuation - Employer branding (recruitment/ employee)	- Sales premium & volume (online vs. offline sales) - Customer loyalty (retention) - Market share - Profitability (revenue growth)

(Vertical label at left: BRAND PERFORMANCE MEASUREMENT)

* NPS® measures customer experience and predicts business growth

BRAND CHANGE DELIVERY PROCESS

The decision to make evolutionary or revolutionary change for your brand has many implications for your organisation. Factors that drive that decision range from shifting demographics, a change in your business model, mergers and acquisitions (M&A), business goals, budget, and much more.

From our 1200-plus successful client projects, we have honed a robust, overarching methodology for delivering complex branding initiatives. These five-phases of Brand Change also result from clients we've guided through the process successfully:

Our Overarching Approach for Brand Change

PHASE 0 — ASSESSING STATUS QUO
PHASE 1 — GETTING ORGANISED
PHASE 2 — GETTING PREPARED
PHASE 3 — GETTING IT DONE
PHASE 4 — GETTING IT TO LAST

PHASE 0: ASSESSING STATUS QUO – M&A ONLY

For M&A (Mergers & Aquisitions): To migrate the brand or not to migrate the brand—assessing the status quo

PHASE 1: GETTING ORGANISED

Investigate and analyse the current and desired situation

PHASE 2: GETTING PREPARED

Make all necessary internal and external preparations to start the brand change project

PHASE 3: GETTING IT DONE

Implement the new or updated brand elements and identity across all assets

PHASE 4: GETTING IT TO LAST

Ensure the new brand takes hold with all stakeholders, and continues to be monitored and to evolve, delivering on its promise

PHASE 0: ASSESSING STATUS QUO - M&A ONLY

Many organisations have acquired brands and kept them, temporarily or permanently, under their original brand. In order to make an informed decision on if, when, and how to migrate, a thorough study would be conducted. The overall brand architecture should be at the foundation of this study. This strategy is always directly derived from the business goals. The aim of this assessment is to give a clear understanding of the risks and opportunities and to help determine which migration strategy is more suitable for the organisation.

AUDIT	BRAND EQUITY	MARKET RESEARCH	LEGAL CHECK	BRAND PORTFOLIO	CULTURE
Map out all existing brands and trademarks in the acquired company	Assess the current brand equity and highlight risks for possible loss of brand value	Determine current market share, credibility of existing brand, how it is positioned, etc.	Evaluate local legal complexities and assess challenges in existing trademark portfolio	Analyse acquired company's product offering against the broader business strategy	Assess internal culture of the new company and any risks for a full integration

Focus on Brand Migration

Brand change as a result of acquisitions isn't always applicable. This is the reason we call this possible part of the process Phase 0. In most cases, the brand change process begins with Phase 1 instead of Phase 0.

Phase 0 provides guidance and understanding on how to manage the branding aspects of new acquisitions, specifically on:

- Considerations for migrating new acquired businesses to the masterbrand—a specific overarching brand name that serves as the main anchoring point on which all underlying products are based (Investopedia 2017)

* Review of different brand migration scenarios for new acquisitions

* Assessment of the best migration scenarios

* How to get organised for the chosen scenario

Reasons to Migrate

As a general rule, intangible assets are a big portion of the value of M&A deals and, in most cases, brands account for a major part of those assets.

Considering the migration of a new acquisition's brand will depend primarily on how well it fits within the existing brand architecture and strategy. That said, it helps to keep these facts in mind when migrating a newly acquired company to the masterbrand:

* Consolidating brands is a smart way to increase the main organisation's market share and realise value

* Migrating allows for the transfer of the acquired company's brand equity to increase the overall brand value of the masterbrand

* Migration makes sense if the brands belong to a sector where marketing costs may be high and the potential for generating value through segmentation is low; all marketing support will be focused on one global brand with one positioning

* Synergies and more coherent customer experiences can be created

* Bigger, global brands attract more employee talent than local, less well-known brands

Reasons NOT to Migrate

Any of the factors listed below may seem to be insufficient reasons to keep the newly acquired brand separate from the masterbrand. However, they can bring greater complexity to the feasibility of the migration and influence the approach needed to minimise risks.

Grounds to refrain from a brand migration or an aggressive timeline:

- Loss of brand equity of the newly migrated company is possible due to its strong position in specific local markets
- Withdrawing well-known brands that people love could result in a loss of customers and market share
- Acquired company offering does not fit with the masterbrand positioning and/or segmentation
- Quality and/or price of the acquired company's products is not within the main organisation's market segment
- Acquired company has a strong brand culture which will bring internal challenges as a result of the migration

Scenarios for Change

Depending on the complexity and feasibility of the migration, an organisation may consider a specific approach to rebranding a newly acquired company. There are three main strategies that can be used:

DIRECT & AGGRESSIVE	"PHASE-IN/PHASE-OUT"	PERFORMANCE KPIs
Lead time: Short planning phase 3 to 6 months rollout	Lead time: 6 to 12 months Phase-in 12 months Phase-out	Lead time: Flexible transition period 1 to 2 years rollout
- This is a very demanding strategy and the most complex scenario to deliver - It needs high investment to drive a successful communication plan - both for internal and external audiences - Once the migration is planned, execution from beginning of communication until removal of the old brand should take no longer than 3 to 6 months for main brand touchpoints	- In this strategy there is a distinction between both phases - In the phase-in the current brand and the new brand exist for a specific period next to each other - After the transition window the old brand is removed (phased-out) - It's common practice that a phase-in period is between 6 to 12 months and that there is a defined period for the speed of phase-out	- Both brand names are kept for a while—for instance using endorsement—giving consumers and trade time to adjust - This strategy somehow combines current brands within the same brand portfolio, and it's less dominant than the Phase-in/Phase-out strategy as it's applied over a longer period of time - However, at some point, one brand will take over the other completely

Complex Brand Migration Scenarios

Two important factors influence the migration strategy and its planning: Regional versus International, and Company Brands versus Product Brands

- Market share, competition, customer loyalty, etc. may differ from one country or region to another
- The migration strategy may need to be tailored differently to each country or region to ensure brand equity and market share are not lost
- The best strategy may consider different scenarios for different markets

- The brand migration strategy should consider the acquired company's brand portfolio as a whole
- Depending on where the brand equity lies, different strategies may be planned for Company Brands versus Product Brands
- Different strategies may be needed for different Product Brands in the portfolio

Complex Brand Migration Scenarios: Planning Map Example

Challenging migration scenarios will usually result in complex rollout programmes. For global organisations, clusters of countries may need to adapt strategies to ensure relevance to their local markets. Here's an example of how the timeline of a complex migration might be mapped.

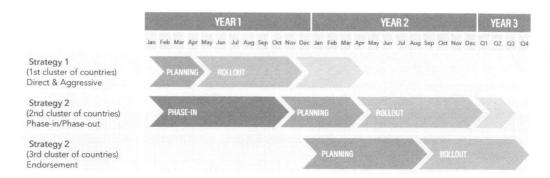

PHASE 1: GETTING ORGANISED

In this phase, we conduct a series of key, centralised stakeholder interviews and information gathering sessions to set the objectives and business administration criteria, in order to explore and understand:

- Organisational structure plus roles and responsibilities, including approval criteria
- Inventory of assets by brand touchpoint areas
- Budget requirements (accounting, centralised/decentralised, etc.)
- Business case requirements to take forward into full rollout
- Operational requirements—form & function
- Assessment of digital functionalities
- Rollout planning for the touchpoints and channels: milestones/programmes
- Identification of synergies and opportunities to combine with other internal initiatives
- Any legacy/framework or contract agreements in place with suppliers or brands

These activities are combined in an Impact Analysis report, providing senior management with the appropriate considerations regarding their choices for scenarios to rebrand.

Impact Analysis Deliverables

Impact of the rebranding from a financial (F), visual (V), and operational (O) perspective includes:

- Overview of key findings obtained during the information gathering process
- Potential issues and risks, including recommended mitigations when rebranding
- Identified areas for savings and process improvements

Feasibility of scenarios for the implementation of the new brand within the organisation.

Priority matrix, in which the degree of visibility/impact of brand touch-points are plotted against the complexity of change

Project budget for the rebranding project, based on the preferred scenario with 85 percent accuracy to include:

- Budget details for the next phases, i.e. definition phase/ specification
- Indicative budgets for subsequent phases

Recommendations, amongst others:

- Time, required budget, savings, and impact opportunities, from a F, V & O (financial, visual, and operational) perspective
- Proposed set-up for the project governance and project organisation including acceptance, escalation and risk management

Priority Matrix

The touchpoint priority matrix provides insight into potential quick wins. It identifies which brand touchpoints can be simply adapted to the new identity to create high visual impact. Depending on the available budget and the time constraints and/or resources, a decision can be made, for example, to go for maximum visual impact or to focus on those touch-points which are easy to convert, but do not necessarily create the most visual impact.

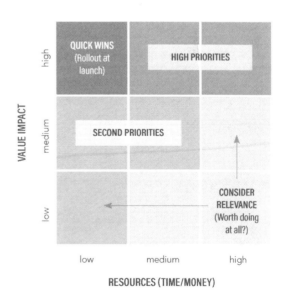

PHASE 2: GETTING PREPARED

After having chosen a preferred rollout scenario, this second phase is about preparing for the forthcoming launch and rollout.

The project moves from strategic and tactical to operational. Creating the project set-up describing roles and responsibilities, availing resources, devising detailed plans, and selecting vendors and suppliers for all work-streams are all part of this phase.

The Project Office during this phase focuses on:

- Structuring the project organisation, reporting and communication channels; escalation, acceptance, and more
- Following Phase 1, deep dive into brand touchpoints where required
- Establishment and/or refinement of reporting, acceptance, change/deviation and escalation procedures
- Risk analysis, including mitigations
- Programme of Requirements (PoR)—priority planning and development of frameworks for all brand touchpoints, including category-specific project plans (process, budget, timelines)
- Design intent interpretation and realisation
- Supplier sourcing and selection—centralised versus localised— ascertaining the best results for the organisation
- Overall management of the project-monitoring progress in each area

Project Set-Up and Planning

Establish the project organisation

- Define roles and responsibilities
- Create and establish the internal workstream teams (marketing, facilities, communications, digital, etc.)
- Establish and/or refine the acceptance, change/deviation, risk, and escalation procedures

- Establish working parameters as a key brand advisory member of the team working closely with the Project Sponsor
- Agree upon and set up the consultation and reporting schedule

Create the initial master planning and continually develop and evolve throughout this phase

- Create the roadmap and highlight any opportunities, risks, and constraints
- Align the creative process timelines, deliverables, and key milestones alongside the master planning

Sense check and verify all previously gathered information across the brand touchpoints, respective impact calculations, and time scenarios to ensure all are still valid and current

Deep dive into the brand touchpoints where further information is required to fully understand the impact

Assess priority planning across brand touchpoints

The graphic below represents sequence of actions for Phases 1 to 4:

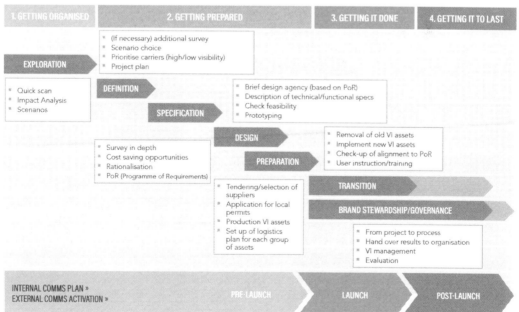

The actual runtime of a brand change programme can be from three months to a few years, depending on the extent of the scope and the desired level of impact.

Project Organisation

A well defined and structured Project Organisation is fundamental to optimising a rebrand programme. Setting up includes defining the criteria of the roles, tasks and responsibilities, and recognising those attributes within the team to onboard them into their forthcoming roles.

A well defined and structured Project Organisation is fundamental to optimising a rebrand programme

During Phase 1, Getting Organised, initial recommendations on the Project Organisation would be made. At the start of Phase 2, Getting Prepared, the Project Organisation will be fully defined, as the preferred scenario for rollout is known by then.

- The Project Organisation should incorporate a Project Management Office (PMO) in which the brand's programme manager (lead) is positioned

- How the rest of the roles are filled is dependent on the capacity of those within the organisation who own the brand touchstream workstreams, what attributes they have for the criteria required, and how an organisation needs to be supported on this non-business-as-usual programme

- Once structure is formed, no matter how small or large the task or programme, it should always define who sits at the strategic, tactical, and operational level; this creates clear communication channels, and enables lateral working collaboration and sharing of best practices

The Project Organisation is the vehicle through which the following core project governance components are managed:

- Status reporting
- Escalation
- Decision making and acceptance
- Deviations or change management
- Risk mitigation including management of constraints

This is a collaborative approach, with lateral and vertical communication, and it is an opportunity that can be capitalised on to engage, empower, and excite colleagues about the forthcoming brand change.

Project Office Ongoing Activities

The project managers, in conjunction with brand touchpoint workstream teams, are responsible for:

- Development of frameworks for the brand touchpoint category-specific project plans (process, budget, timelines, etc.)
- Approval and buy-in of project plans for each brand touchpoint category
- Development of the Programme of Requirements, as input for the development of the applied designs
- Development of the brand touchpoint-specific applied designs
- Consultation (where required) with procurement and/or workstream teams regarding supplier sourcing and selection (or within existing contracts)
- Various brand touchpoint category-specific actions

Indicative roles and responsibilities of work process during brand change are shown on the following page.

Indicative roles and responsibilities of work process during brand change.

PHASE 1: GETTING ORGANISED

- Brand development & information gathering
- Centralised approach with business and regions just as consults (grey outline boxes)
- Small project team to safeguard confidentiality
- External trusted partners to support internal teams

PHASE 2 & 3: GETTING PREPARED & GETTING IT DONE

- Brand activation & launch/rollout preparations
- Phases are driven centrally with regions responsible for the delivery
- Project organisation is responsible for instigating brand stewardship for next phase

PHASE 4: GETTING IT TO LAST

- New brand stewardship is put in place
- Small global PMO team hands over the outcome of the rebrand to the new stewards
- Local project offices hand over to local brand and marketing teams

Sourcing Strategy

A crucial step in the brand change process is to identify the sourcing strategy, in conjunction with your colleagues from Procurement. Assessing whether the existing network of vendors and suppliers can be used or not is key. Prior to doing so, you need to identify which brand touchpoint categories would have to be addressed centrally, regionally, or locally.

Additional activities in this phase consist of:

- Applying the intelligence gathered during Phase 1, Getting Organised, to tailor the methodology; defining the correct tendering and purchasing process; assessing a central versus local approach; or establishing a combination approach including local and central regulations, permits and policies such as permissions, laws, and sustainability

- Defining the change as a result of Phase 1 to incorporate budget, ambition, desired timeline—those parameters should be considered when establishing needs and requirements, selecting suppliers, and managing contracts

- Purchasing brand and corporate identity assets (such as IT support, printed materials, signage, wayfinding, and digital tooling) which not only require knowledge of the technology used, sustainability, maintenance requirements, and visual appearance, market prices, guarantees, liabilities, and conditions for cost-effective solutions

Procurement Process

Our typical roles and responsibilities in the procurement process:

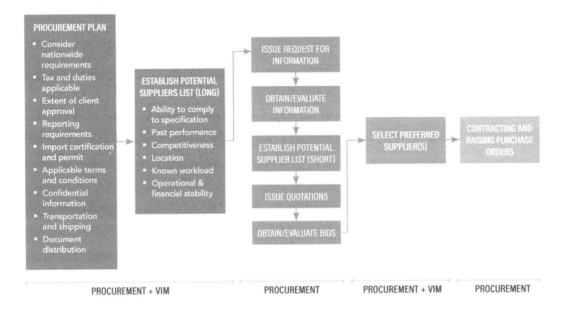

Typical roles and responsibilities throughout the rollout of the visual identity application process:

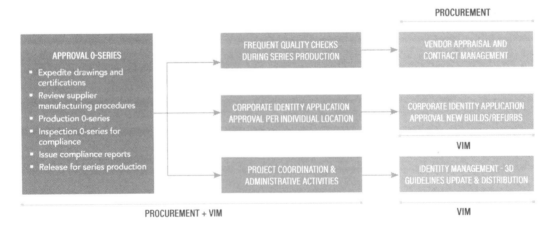

CI refers to Corporate Identity in the graphics

PHASE 3: GETTING IT DONE

In this phase, the planning and preparation activities from Phase 2 would be applied. The primary focus in this phase is the actual implementation of the concept. This includes:

- Ongoing monitoring, steering, and support from the Project Office, which involves resolving issues, dealing with escalation and decision-making, across all workstreams

- Agreeing on the structure and format for future rollout and subsequent supplier tendering in conjunction with the initial set of concept guidelines and applied designs

- Execution of supplier and vendor works, if necessary, depending on the project needs

- Monitoring and managing the production and/or implementation programme for all brand touchpoints

- Starting to build a management and maintenance structure for post-implementation, which involves aligning with the brand management/stewardship process deployed during the first two phases

PHASE 4: GETTING IT TO LAST

After a significant rebranding effort—both in time and money—the primary focus of this stage is to ensure the brand is truly embedded within the organisation through both physical and emotional consistency after the initial launch.

We recommend setting up a management and maintenance structure for post-implementation brand stewardship. Ambitions and goals should be assessed and defined and should be dependent on the scale and scope of the change. This structure includes people, processes, and tools. Examples include:

- Brand ambassadors (people and process)
- Brand council—enabling a communication method to facilitate brand questions and auditing (people and process)
- A central Webshop/creation centre for branded assets (process and tools), including image bank, app, marketing asset bank, printing-on-demand (business cards, posters, brochures, etc.)
- Asset management - central database for all locations (tools), including address and contact details, signage inventory, pictures, relevant documents, i.e. planning permission, etc.
- Management reporting, including brand measurement and quantification (people, process and tools)

Process to Create the Structure

INTAKE & INTERVIEW AUDIT	BUILDING BLOCKS	DEFINITION OF ROLES & RESPONSIBILITIES	PROCESSES & TOOLS	BRAND STEWARDSHIP IMPLEMENTATION PLAN

DISCOVER & DEVELOP	IMPLEMENT

- Define the scope - Define existing structures - Develop interview questions - Analyse outcome and define gaps - Gap analysis and audit report	- Brand steward-ship, strategy, and structure - Define depart-ments, people, and tools involved - Budget allocation - High level tasks & responsibilities	- Develop roles and responsibil-ities at all three levels (strategic, tactical, and operational) - Develop imple-mentation model	- Define processes - Select appro-priate tools to support the people and the processes	- Implement processes and tools

AN OVERVIEW OF DIGITAL ENABLERS AND MANAGEMENT TOOLS

To ensure this book is as comprehensive as possible, we are including an overview of four digital enablers and management tools:

ImpactValuator™

ImpactValuator is the unique instrument that helps to gauge the cost, rollout scenarios, and potential savings of a (re)brand with 70-75 percent accuracy. It's normally applied as part of an Impact Analysis. Our database consists of hundreds of cases, gathered over the last fifteen years, incorporating data across all sectors and sizes of companies.

Basically, our ImpactValuator enables a brand to gauge the level of investment for a potential rebrand during the early stage of consideration.

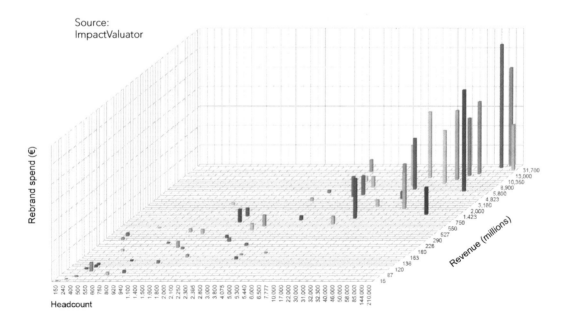

Source:
ImpactValuator

To apply the ImpactValuator, only two parameters are needed to come up with quick results: revenue and headcount. When we have this information for a specific organisation, we're able to pull the appropriate data from our database, containing hundreds of reference cases that we've been gathering over the years. The approach is based on statistics in the database, and a review of how the new identity will be applied, from outside to inside the organisation. This helps in facilitating initial conversations with senior management.

Brand Performance Scan

We reviewed the Brand Performance Scan in Step 0 of our Brand Improvement Process. However, it is important to go over it again here, since it is such an important aspect of building and maintaining brand value. You may remember that the Brand Performance Scan is based on the Brand Life Cycle Model.

In order to make informed decisions on improving your brand performance, we developed the Brand Performance Scan. The Brand Performance Scan provides data-driven insights on the quality of current brand management (within the organisation), brand manifestation, and brand performance.

We assess how the brand touchpoints deliver on the brand promise, and identify which internal factors influence the brand performance.

Quantitative and qualitative data will be collected via desk research, online questionnaires will be administered, and stakeholder interviews will be conducted. The data contains information on:

- Role of the brand within the organisation
- Current brand governance organisation
- Processes and assets
- Available tools (KPIs, guidelines, and brand management systems)
- Budgets and total cost of ownership

The Brand Performance Scan is based on the Brand Life Cycle Model.

BRAND LIFE CYCLE MODEL

BRAND MANAGEMENT

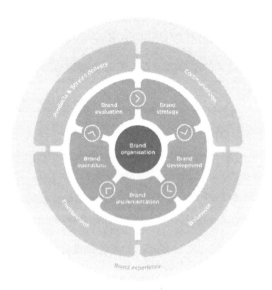
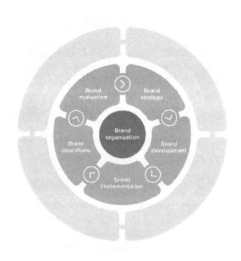

Measurement:

Maturity of brand management
organisation related to brand
documentation, processes, tools,
systems, and instruments

With the tools and resources to carry out the audit, improvements are localised and translated to actionable initiatives. In our view, the most important reason to translate the findings of the scan is to develop a comprehensive roadmap for brand improvement. By means of a dashboard, both the current situation, as well as changes since previous measurements, are reported.

Brand2Manage™

Brand2Manage is the online platform and support desk to manage the multinational workflow and fulfilment of 3D-branded assets across territories around the world. For example, the global rebrand of all signage and

BRAND MANIFESTATION

BRAND PERFORMANCE

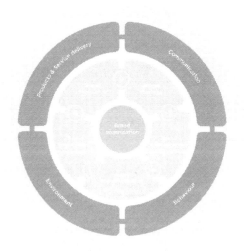

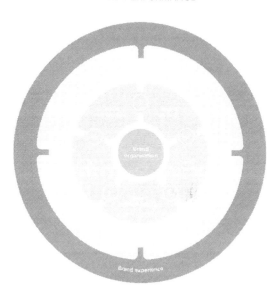

Measurement:

Consistency, coherency, quality, and fit of brand promise with the visual and verbal messages at select brand touchpoints

Measurement:

Brand experience per target audience: awareness, associations, attitude, and behaviour

interiors for Merck is managed with Brand2Manage. The online platform provides central control and management information, and facilitates local rollout with all suppliers, internal stakeholders, and local municipalities involved. This results in substantial savings during the work process, as human intervention is minimised.

Brand Portals

This is an ever-evolving space, so we'll elaborate our thoughts on Brand Portals in the article on the following page.

Brand portals must be anchored as one of the core processes of an organisation

Traditionally brand portals are not considered to be part of an organisation's core processes. The corporate communications or brand management teams are often the owners of the brand portal, and they usually don't encourage their usage effectively to the wider company or integrate it into the organisation's digital ecosystem.

For example, colleagues who sit within the design, marketing, and sales departments often need to access brand assets during their daily routines. This access could be easily facilitated by integrating the portal within other relevant applications.

It is often the case that the designated person with the role of maintaining the content of the brand portal doesn't regularly update content or add metadata—information that provides details about other data—to improve the UI/UX (user experience/user interface) and activate user groups. This results in colleagues being unable to find the content they need, or to even know that the portal exists. The relevance of the portal declines over time, and eventually becomes obsolete.

From stand-alone brand portal to integrated hub

If you switch to a Hub solution, the function of the brand portal lives on. You can still facilitate the use and downloads of the logo and photography, as well as the downloading or ordering of marketing materials, such as business cards and brochures. This is accompanied by a well thought-out workflow which helps to streamline processes.

However, a typical brand portal is not sufficiently integrated into the organisation's digital ecosystem. Photographs and marketing materials are stored separately in the many different Web (Content) Management Systems (W(C)MS) for websites, apps, intranet systems, etc. This can waste time spent searching for assets, and it is difficult to maintain control of the branded content.

For example, by setting up your brand portal as a Hub, you are able to publish a brochure directly to your W(C)MS. This is the best way to keep centralised access to your materials, and to make sure that everyone is using the most up-to-date versions of those assets. Have a new version of a brochure? Customise it in your brand portal. Thanks to the Hub function, it is immediately available everywhere!

A practical example of integration in the core process: PIM

Product Information Management (PIM) systems are the spider in the web between the data coming from the ERP (Enterprise Resource Planning) package. Those include prices or product information and related content such as packaging and photography. All this data is then directly used in the e-commerce platform. It is an integrated digital highway, at the core of your brand management process.

Wouldn't it be great if you could upload all your photography and marketing materials, and then your brand portal publishes to all digital channels including the website? That would result in the brand manager being in control of all digital brand touchpoints. This dream is more realistic than you might think. In addition, thanks to the explosion of digital channels, it's now easier to maintain a coherent brand image.

Maintenance of the next generation brand portals will take a lot more effort. Proper content and metadata won't be a minor issue anymore, but crucial to well-functioning processes.

Give maximum support to the users of the portal

Of course, it's not only publishing to digital channels that matters. The design department needs the brand guidelines and photography, and sales colleagues also want to use the best photography in their PowerPoint presentations to impress their prospective clients. Are these groups actively involved in the brand portal? What content do they need exactly? By creating user personas, you can easily map the content needs of your target groups, and you can ensure that everything is relevant for both your internal and external audiences. To facilitate these user groups, the content and the metadata need to be kept up-to-date, otherwise users won't be able to find what they're looking for in the brand portal.

The brand portal contributes to a stronger brand

The brand strategy is fully integrated into the organisation when the brand portal is anchored into the core processes. As a direct result, the touchpoints will always be on-brand, saving time and money for colleagues who use the brand assets. In short, a well-executed brand portal contributes to a stronger brand.

PART 4
LEARNING
FROM
EXAMPLES

An organisation must continually evolve. If it doesn't, it's actually standing still, and getting left behind. Your brand is your business enabler, with an important, central role in your organisation's success. It must be monitored when subtle or perhaps profound changes are needed.

With the rise of digital technology, sustaining meaningful brand connections and positive customer experiences across multiple channels is essential. In this part of the book, we'll show you a few anonymous client examples to demonstrate some specific dynamics and magnitudes in brand change programmes.

Project Type, Scope, and Service Summaries

These select examples are from four different sectors. Each case shows a range of options which may apply to your organisation if you are considering a possible rebrand.

In selecting these examples, we considered the following:

- The extent of change (from evolutionary to revolutionary)
- Size of the projects
- Projects with a global footprint
- Chosen timelines and rollout strategy
- Mix of B2B and B2C organisations

We also noted the lessons learnt from the examples to help you avoid mistakes, whilst benefiting from what was done successfully.

Example: Brand Touchpoint Priority Matrix for a Financial Services Brand

The brand touchpoint priority matrix can provide insight into potential quick wins. In this instance, we identified which touchpoints could be simply adapted to the new identity, thereby creating high visual impact versus other touchpoints that would require more effort to implement with greater financial impact.

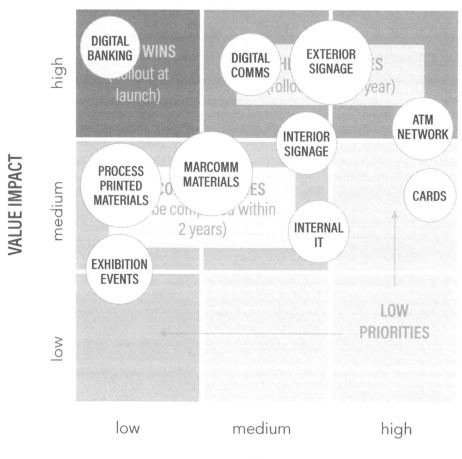

Financial Services Example:
Brand Revitalisation

Background:
Newly created brand for global banking company

Ambition level:

- New logo

- New visual identity

- No name change

- Digital-ready identity

- Evolutionary process

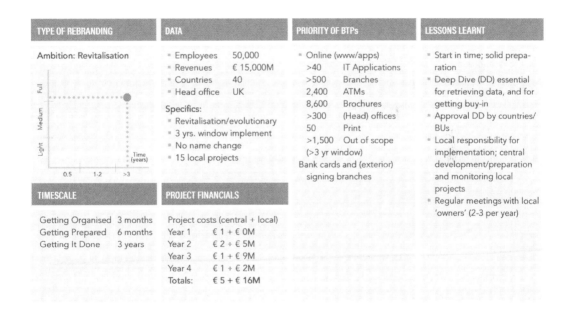

TYPE OF REBRANDING	DATA	PRIORITY OF BTPs	LESSONS LEARNT
Ambition: Revitalisation	Employees 50,000 Revenues € 15,000M Countries 40 Head office UK Specifics: Revitalisation/evolutionary 3 yrs. window implement No name change 15 local projects	Online (www/apps) >40 IT Applications >500 Branches 2,400 ATMs 8,600 Brochures >300 (Head) offices 50 Print >1,500 Out of scope (>3 yr window) Bank cards and (exterior) signing branches	Start in time; solid prepa-ration Deep Dive (DD) essential for retrieving data, and for getting buy-in Approval DD by countries/BUs Local responsibility for implementation; central development/preparation and monitoring local projects Regular meetings with local 'owners' (2-3 per year)

TIMESCALE	PROJECT FINANCIALS
Getting Organised 3 months Getting Prepared 6 months Getting It Done 3 years	Project costs (central + local) Year 1 € 1 + € 0M Year 2 € 2 + € 5M Year 3 € 1 + € 9M Year 4 € 1 + € 2M Totals: € 5 + € 16M

Aviation Project Example: Rebranding of Divisions

Background:
The aim was to unify the company's branding and create a more monolithic brand architecture (structure)

Ambition level:

- New brand architecture

- Name and logo change for some divisions and groups

- Fairly quick rollout program

- Logical step for the outer world with gradual change

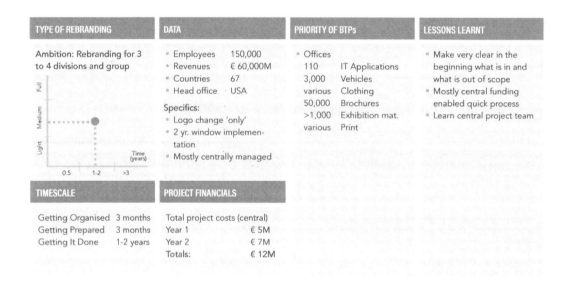

TYPE OF REBRANDING	DATA	PRIORITY OF BTPs	LESSONS LEARNT
Ambition: Rebranding for 3 to 4 divisions and group	Employees 150,000 Revenues € 60,000M Countries 67 Head office · USA **Specifics:** Logo change 'only' 2 yr. window implementation Mostly centrally managed	Offices 110 IT Applications 3,000 Vehicles various Clothing 50,000 Brochures >1,000 Exhibition mat. various Print	Make very clear in the beginning what is in and what is out of scope Mostly central funding enabled quick process Learn central project team

TIMESCALE		PROJECT FINANCIALS	
Getting Organised	3 months	Total project costs (central)	
Getting Prepared	3 months	Year 1	€ 5M
Getting It Done	1-2 years	Year 2	€ 7M
		Totals:	€ 12M

Pharmaceutical Company Example:
Full Rebrand, No Name Change

Background:
The goal was to transform the business from pharma
to pharma-tech company

Ambition level:

* Global rebrand, with a revolutionary new design for this sector
  and a large visual and business impact

* In the run up to launch, the brand team consisted of three
  external resources and six internal resources

* Post launch, the core brand team included about six people

* Divisions and functions built their own project teams to deliver
  their specific touchpoints with the most important areas having
  at least part-time colleagues allocated to the rebrand

* A Central Programme Office managed the full rebrand,
  tracking and communicating progress to senior stakeholders
  and the project's steering group

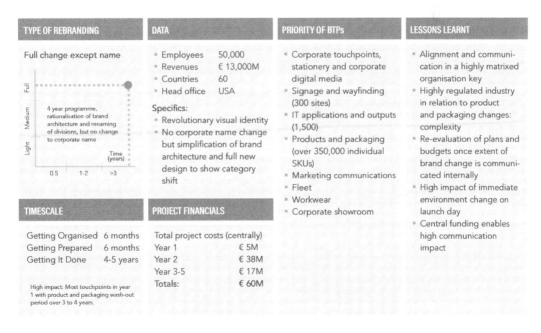

TYPE OF REBRANDING	DATA	PRIORITY OF BTPs	LESSONS LEARNT
Full change except name	▪ Employees 50,000 ▪ Revenues € 13,000M ▪ Countries 60 ▪ Head office USA Specifics: ▪ Revolutionary visual identity ▪ No corporate name change but simplification of brand architecture and full new design to show category shift	▪ Corporate touchpoints, stationery and corporate digital media ▪ Signage and wayfinding (300 sites) ▪ IT applications and outputs (1,500) ▪ Products and packaging (over 350,000 individual SKUs) ▪ Marketing communications ▪ Fleet ▪ Workwear ▪ Corporate showroom	▪ Alignment and communication in a highly matrixed organisation key ▪ Highly regulated industry in relation to product and packaging changes: complexity ▪ Re-evaluation of plans and budgets once extent of brand change is communicated internally ▪ High impact of immediate environment change on launch day ▪ Central funding enables high communication impact

(chart within TYPE OF REBRANDING panel: 4 year programme, rationalisation of brand architecture and renaming of divisions, but no change to corporate name. Axes: Light / Medium / Full vs Time (years) 0.5, 1-2, >3)

TIMESCALE		PROJECT FINANCIALS	
Getting Organised	6 months	Total project costs (centrally)	
Getting Prepared	6 months	Year 1	€ 5M
Getting It Done	4-5 years	Year 2	€ 38M
		Year 3-5	€ 17M
		Totals:	€ 60M

High impact: Most touchpoints in year
1 with product and packaging wash-out
period over 3 to 4 years.

Chemical Sciences Company Example: Full Rebrand, No Name Change

Background:
The goal was to transform the business from chemical sciences to materials and life cycle sector

Ambition level:

- Global rebrand, with a revolutionary new design for this sector and a large visual and business impact

- Launch event for employees in cinemas with a 45-minute movie explaining the new brand

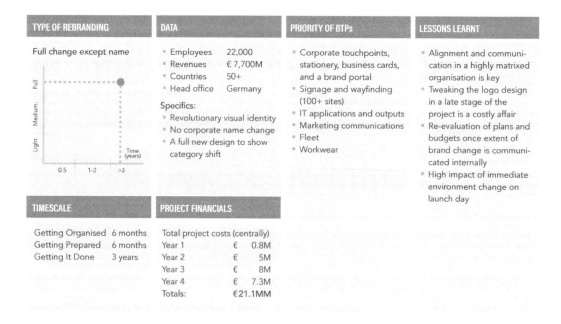

TYPE OF REBRANDING	DATA	PRIORITY OF BTPs	LESSONS LEARNT
Full change except name	Employees 22,000 Revenues € 7,700M Countries 50+ Head office Germany Specifics: Revolutionary visual identity No corporate name change A full new design to show category shift	Corporate touchpoints, stationery, business cards, and a brand portal Signage and wayfinding (100+ sites) IT applications and outputs Marketing communications Fleet Workwear	Alignment and communication in a highly matrixed organisation is key Tweaking the logo design in a late stage of the project is a costly affair Re-evaluation of plans and budgets once extent of brand change is communicated internally High impact of immediate environment change on launch day

TIMESCALE		PROJECT FINANCIALS	
Getting Organised	6 months	Total project costs (centrally)	
Getting Prepared	6 months	Year 1	€ 0.8M
Getting It Done	3 years	Year 2	€ 5M
		Year 3	€ 8M
		Year 4	€ 7.3M
		Totals:	€21.1MM

Our 1200-plus client examples effectively demonstrate the importance of smart implementation and continuous management to build and sustain brand performance and marketplace value. They serve as examples from which lessons can be learned. They also demonstrate how they have established vibrant, engaging brands that their customers can connect with in a powerful way. You can view them at vim-group.com to see which might be relevant to your own anticipated project.

PART 5
FAQs: ASKING AND ANSWERING THE RIGHT QUESTIONS

133   What is brand implementation?

135   Don't branding agencies offer implementation services?

137   What are the steps involved in brand implementation, and what services do you provide?

140   What is the most effective way to build a case for a potential rebrand?

141   What are the reasons you see organisations take on rebranding?

142   What typical mistakes do you see organisations make around their rebrand, implementation, or even their rollout?

143 What changes have you seen in your work with the evolving touchpoints and channels?

145 Who do you typically work with in companies?

146 How can companies find savings and optimise results with their rebranding initiative?

148 How would you improve brand management within organisations?

149 What changes and trends do you see with brands navigating change?

We receive a number of questions that we believe have been addressed in previous parts of this book. However, due to the frequency with which these questions arise, we wanted to highlight a few here, making it easier for you to connect the specific question with the pertinent response. We recommend that you review other parts of the book, most specifically Part 3, in which our work processes are outlined in greater detail.

As you plan your brand change, we have also created additional free resources for learning at our website. There, you will see a few more frequently asked questions with answers that will help you with your brand change, in addition to other valuable information. Plans for ongoing additions and updates to those resources will be freely available to you. Please refer to the Resources section or contact us directly.

For now, here are answers to the common questions we receive.

Q What is brand implementation?

A Brand implementation is the entire process of converting a creative idea into reality across all touchpoints and all channels. If you are more narrowly focused, it's about how you can translate elements of visual identity into reality. It includes how to apply the design and brand elements in digital environments, such as websites, apps, mobile, or IT systems; print materials; buildings and other 3-D environments like retail spaces; pertinent exterior environments, signage, and wayfinding solutions; fleet and all equipment; and wearables, such as uniforms.

Basically, we do two things: we help our clients to implement their brands, and we help them to manage their brands. That management is primarily about putting a governance team and process in place to ensure the investment in the brand is optimised. Doing so means you will be better prepared to increase the brand's value over time, drive positive client or customer interactions, and prepare for inevitable future change. Accomplishing this requires a series of actions and capabilities to bring brand experiences to life. As emphasised throughout this book, this includes creativity, advanced strategy, data-driven insights, logistics, predictive analytics, and an effective management framework.

> Put a governance team and process in place to ensure the investment in the brand is optimised

Most importantly, you need those with expertise on how to deliver and manage your brand change. You'll need support with a proven process—how to organise the work to be done, plan and schedule the steps involved, and develop the right budget; all with a strategy for successful delivery and ongoing management.

It is important to access benchmark information pertaining to scoping, budgeting, structuring your ideal team and finding the best agencies for your efforts, as well as coordinating and managing the right set of partners and vendors. Amongst the top questions when contemplating brand change are: How do we build the business case? How do we budget properly for this? Are there ways we can save money? Is there a feasible rollout? How can we ensure our employees are included and integrated in this process? How do we make sure clients, customers, and prospects embrace the results? How can we drive more marketplace value from our investment?

These are just a few of the many aspects of brand implementation and management we help you address. When done right, the entire process results in net positive for your entire organisation and helps to drive your marketplace success.

It is important to work with professionals experienced in your sector and at your scale. Making a major brand change is rare, so you will increase your chances for success if you are properly prepared. Work with a team with past experience that you can learn from to avoid costly mistakes. Having access to their insights and relevant data that can apply to your own organisation will increase your likelihood of maximising ROI.

Q Don't branding agencies offer implementation services?

A The services we provide are a 100 percent complementary fit with branding agencies. In fact, many of the world's leading agencies consult with us and ask us to partner with them on various projects. VIM Group is neither a strategic brand or design consultancy, nor a product supplier. Consider our capabilities delivered from an objective position:

- We are advisors, programme and project managers, and specialists with deep knowledge in all specific brand applications

- We are an independent company, enabling us to provide an objective view to get the job done in the simplest possible way within the constraints of the brand and our clients' objectives

- Our competitive edge is that we deliver consultancy project management and expertise across all brand touchpoints and branded assets

- Having successfully conducted over 1200 brand implementation projects, our capabilities are such that we ensure brand coherence and an efficient, timely, and cost-effective execution

- We are proficient at applying our services internationally or at a national/country-specific level, and our suite of digital tools ensure optimal brand management and implementation across organisations

Part 3 of this book will help you understand our roles and how we complement agencies, your internal teams, and vendors with methodologies for delivering your brand change.

We focus on the business administration side of bringing your brand change to life. You can also say that agencies create the magic, and we provide the logic.

If you were to draw an analogy with buildings, agencies would be the architects, and we would be the construction management company overseeing, planning, and preparing all that need to be done to get the structures built. Since ongoing efforts are required to retain that magic internally and externally, we continue helping you with brand management. This essential process ensures you raise and sustain your level of brand performance and marketplace value.

You know you need an entity with the big ideas on positioning strategy and design. However, you might also recognise that expertise in coordinating internal and external entities is required in order to bring these ideas to life and to drive results.

This graphic depicts our areas of responsibilities as compared to those typically provided by agencies:

	AUDIT AND STRATEGY	PLAN AND PRODUCE	ROLLOUT AND MANAGE
VIM GROUP	Audits; Budgets & timeline; Agency selection; Rationalisation; Value engineering; Process improvement; Vendor strategies; Project organisation	Transition strategies; Industrial design; Technical specifications; Application; Procurement; Detailed transition plans; Implementation tools; RFP development	Project management; Reporting; Manufacturing & installation; Supervision; Process automation; Digital asset management; Brand management tools; Asset maintenance; Brand management organisation
BRANDING AGENCY	Brand strategy; Identity/logo design; Brand architecture; Brand guidelines; Brand platform; Brand messaging	Application guidelines; Marketing & advertising; Corporate communications; Brand tools; Websites	Brand culture & training; Launch events

Q What are the steps involved in brand implementation, and what services do you provide?

A For any branding update, we first determine if the planned change will be evolutionary or revolutionary. This helps us with the scoping of potential scenarios, project budget, and how we customise our delivery methodology to achieve success.

Some companies merge, buy, or sell a portion of the organisation. That has revolutionary implications. The official identity will change. There will be more dramatic shifts required within your organisation and at various points of contact for your customers and prospects. Often, these involve regulatory changes, legal assessments, and risk assessments. In a number of instances there is the need to create a new name. You can imagine that the business drivers for such profound change must be sound, given the potential impact on time and resources to be invested.

Here's how we define an evolutionary type of change: gradual change of your brand and identity and a change in your communications style without changing the logo. Maybe your colour palette will be adapted, and your style of images and photography may shift a bit.

These are the types of changes that involve evolutionary migration of brand elements. They are smaller, less dramatic adjustments in the way you express your brand.

Most companies know they are in an ever-changing marketplace. Either their current positions no longer reflect who they are, or they are preparing for their next phase. They want to express that not only in their competitive landscape, but also as they work to build and maintain relevance for their internal and external audiences.

Whether your brand change is evolutionary or revolutionary, we apply our proprietary process. A prior Phase 0, Assessing the Status Quo, is included specifically for migration of brands as a result of an acquisition.

Our phased delivery process is addressed in greater detail in Part 3 of this book. However, here is an overview of the four typical phases: Phase 1 is Getting Organised, and Phase 2 is Getting Prepared. Those two first phases lead up to the moment of launch. Then from the launch, we have Phase 3, which is Getting It Done. This is the execution work beyond the day-one launch with the rollout of brand elements, which can last from several months to several years, depending on the budget and goals, and related scenario option selected.

Phase 4 is Getting It to Last, which is continual. This last phase is more about brand management, which incorporates ongoing monitoring of brand performance with alerts on where and when change is needed.

Let's go back to Phase 1, Getting Organised. From a brand owner's perspective, thinking about a new brand strategy or revitalisation, a number of questions will come to mind: First, what will be the implications in terms of finances, money, investment, and costs? Second, how do I need to get organised to get this done successfully? Third, will there be any synergies or opportunities that we can leverage by doing something like this?

You can plan for revolutionary impact, but if the investment implications are not affordable, then you might need to pull back. Framing the options for rollout in terms of time, speed, and ambition level also plays a role in your decisions.

To scope costs, we have a database that we have been building over the last fifteen years. With our database and proprietary corresponding tool, the ImpactValuator, we have the ability to gauge rebranding costs with about 70 percent to 80 percent accuracy. This tool also helps us map out financial impact across the various scenarios.

Big goals are great. However, with a better idea of the investment level required, you will be able to determine the best way to have your brand change implemented most effectively across the organisation. This will help you devise a more effective project plan and to structure the necessary team to execute it. How many people will you need internally? How much of their time should be dedicated to this effort? How well prepared or capable is the organisation, and what kind of external support will be necessary?

Phase 4, Getting It to Last, with a focus on overall aspects of brand management, is critical. Yet, it is the phase that organisations often exclude or fail to budget for and incorporate. The phase involves monitoring of the brand within a governance framework. With an ongoing brand performance review, you will be provided with real-time data and insights and future-focused analytics, so you will know when and how to update or evolve your brand.

Q What is the most effective way to build a case for a potential rebrand?

A When building a case for a rebrand, the biggest challenge we see is the varying focus between those typically in charge of the brand within organisations (brand, marketing, and communication groups) and those from whom approval for funds and business/positioning strategy (boardroom) is needed. Fortunately, board directors are showing increased understanding and interest in how their organisations interact with customers and the ensuing business value driver that these interactions can be.

When making your case to this audience, provide evidence via examples you have researched and identified. In fact, some stats in this book could be helpful.

Many corporate board members have earned their positions by excelling in more traditional, quantitatively measured roles. Whilst marketing and brand-speak is about how to engage, convert, and win customers, boardroom language is more focused on business cases, strategies, rationale, and figures. Keep your case for your rebrand clear, focused, and present in a language of the audience from whom you want to secure a buy-in.

Q What are the reasons you see organisations take on rebranding?

A Organisations we work with rebrand for a range of reasons. Some are carving and selling off parts of their companies. Others are slipping in the marketplace and need to strengthen their position to become more competitive. A number have to reset or revise their business models as a result of lowered barriers to entry in their industry sector or shifting demographics in our age of digital transformation.

Each organisation has its unique reasons for taking on brand change. We encourage you to start with an audit of your current state and understand the full investment required before making the very important decision to go forward. It is better to understand the internal and external implications as well as the opportunities that effectively planned, delivered, and managed brand change can provide. Please see more at Reasons for Brand Change in Part 2.

Q What typical mistakes do you see organisations make around their rebrand, implementation, or even their rollout?

A Five or even seven years ago, you could imagine your messaging and then roll it out. You would tell your internal team what you were doing and why you were doing it, and you would synchronise that position with your actions and statements in the external world.

Those days are gone. Yet many brands still operate as if they have full control of the story and narrative around their brands. If you continue with that stance today, the social media sphere which can include anonymous voices from your internal team, will expose whatever you're attempting to cover up.

Inside-out should be the main approach. In addition, there has been a massive change in channels and how to engage with customers and prospects. Some brands are too heavily branded, meaning that they still believe they succeed by placing their identity everywhere, at every opportunity—especially offline. The digital era leads now, yet the tendency to do what we term as overbranding, consistent with the predigital era, seems to continue.

Q What changes have you seen in your work with the evolving touchpoints and channels?

A As we noted in Part 2, the role of a brand is changing in our age of digital transformation and its impact in our world. Let's review:

- New eco-systems are emerging; digital and ad agencies are entering the space of branding, and traditional branding agencies are taking on digital campaigns

- A brand's space to express itself is limited to smaller and smaller screens

- Brand owners are building in-house capability to enable a more agile response to customer demands

There is a shift from consistence to coherence for brands, which is spurred by the digital channels and the need for flexibility in the interpretation of brand elements, especially in smaller spaces.

> You have to continually adapt, try, test, evaluate, and change again

The place to put your name, your logo or your identity is totally different than what it used to be, when putting your logo on a building was the most visible way to represent your brand.

We're living in a world where branding is more about experience and a customer journey. You have to be strategic about ways to make an impression on your customers and internal audiences over time.

That's not necessarily a matter of putting your identity everywhere. It's a matter of prioritising and discovering where the impact is biggest and the effort is the least. This is a different and new dynamic. We now find that with many clients, there are increasing opportunities to spend less on placing brand elements at multiple touchpoints and to spend more on fewer, more effective channels with greater resulting impact.

We would say that any organisation that's continually working on making adjustments to its branding across channels and across journeys has the right and necessary approach these days. Whether that means they are achieving the desired outcomes or not depends on the right strategy and execution mix.

We see an ongoing trend, especially with financial services organisations, of consolidation through acquisitions. Whatever type of brand change you are addressing, agility is the word that's really important here. You have to continually adapt, try, test, evaluate, and change again.

Due to the rise of mobile and smart watches, digital first is the way to go when structuring customer experiences. The growing and evolving impact of digitalisation on when and how customers interact with you is now the primary consideration, even more than interaction in physical spaces for many industry sectors.

Q Who do you typically work with in companies?

A We play a major role in delivering the brand promise of large and SME (small to medium enterprise) organisations, NGOs (non-governmental organisations), corporations, and multinationals whose questions around brand implementation and management topics are complex.

Depending on where branding sits in an organisation and the responsibility of the pertinent C-level leader determine who brings us on board. The person that owns the brand could be the chief marketing officer (CMO) or the corporate communications officer (CCO). Some companies have chief brand officers.

Whichever the title or the specific function, that individual and her or his team are responsible for the corporate brand within an organisation. Our range of typical contacts and key decision makers include:

* Brand managers
* CMOs
* Corporate communications
* Marketing communications
* Facilities
* Increasingly UX/IT managers and business units, due to the digitalisation of the brand

What they all have in common is their demand for a professional, expert-driven approach for brand implementation and management.

Q How can companies find savings and optimise results with their rebranding initiative?

A We find a variety of ways in every instance. We believe this is one of the reasons organisations choose to work with us. Since we are independent from agencies and vendors, our objective priority is your brand.

There are a number of ways organisations can realise savings whilst maximising return on investment for their brand change initiative. Those ways range from building the right business case for the decision to move forward, choosing the right brand consultants as partners, to understanding the true tangible and intangible costs of making the change.

Much depends on the objective of your rebrand, the scope or extent of change required, and your answers to a number of questions. Is it a small or large change? Does it need to be made quickly for some business reason, or can it be phased-in over time? Could you apply your identity at fewer touchpoints? What's the impact on internal resources needed to manage the branding going forward? Can your internal team, even if supplemented with outside groups, devote the necessary resources for the effort?

> Much depends on the objective of your rebrand, the extent of change required

Other places where savings could be realised are through external parties like vendors, suppliers, and agencies. Does the organisation have an appetite to remain working with existing suppliers? Do you want or need to consider new suppliers and vendors that may be more experienced in the direction you would like to go and with the new touchpoint channels to come? Again, an entity without financial stake in your suppliers, vendors, agencies, and other partners is better positioned to help you achieve your goals most cost effectively.

In Part 3, we outlined our overall process for delivering complex brand implementation and management efforts, all based on a goal for efficient, effective ROI. Some of the ways we facilitate savings for brand change are also depicted in this graphic below:

How VIM Group will save money for you whilst safeguarding your brand

STANDARDISATION & RATIONALISATION	Standardisation & rationalisation of brand touchpoints will not only decrease diversity and improve consistency, it will also impact cost efficiency in a positive way through economy of scale in buying.
VALUE ENGINEERING	Optimising the visual appearance and technical design of 3D assets through value engineering, achieving cost efficiency and lowest total cost of ownership.
SOURCING STRATEGY & SUPPLIER/VENDOR TENDERING	Determining number and geographical spread of product suppliers to maximise brand control and minimise additional cost, whilst using our extensive market knowledge to get the best prices for the highest quality.
ROLLOUT STRATEGY	Aligning the rebranding initiative with operational refurbishment schemes to avoid double spending.
BRAND AS MAIN PERSPECTIVE	"Less is more" is one of our main principles. Since we are independent from product suppliers, we have no interest in selling product, which will avoid expensive overbranding.
EXPERIENCE AND EXPERTISE	We have been in business for many years, and more importantly, we have been in this specific business for twenty-five-plus years. We recognise pitfalls and make sure that our clients won't make expensive mistakes.

Q How would you improve brand management within organisations?

A Brand management is an ongoing, ever-evolving process with the goal to optimise brand experience and value. Good brand management is key to the long-term success of your brand, and we believe that you should increase impact, over time, and minimise spending. We work with brands to be coherent and effective on an ongoing basis. The issues we help you address include:

- Brand audits
- Brand performance analysis
- Synchronisation of digital and physical visual identity
- Set-up of future-proof brand stewardship

> Good brand management is key to the long-term success of your brand

In general, we provide you with support, when you need it, to augment your internal organisation and to structure the right team and framework for managing your brand. We combine our proprietary data, unique in the industry, with insightful advice and proven execution on every aspect of your brand management.

What changes and trends do you see with brands navigating change?

 Your Brand Supply Chain

If we liken your brand to a complex supply chain, it begins with smart planning and strategy. If properly aligned with company position, you enable your organisational goals. The result is that your brand manifestation will be done right within the company and at external touchpoints.

Brand as Business Enabler

We believe your brand is your business enabler, and you should organise it as a business tool. Although this is now shifting, the brand is still relegated, for most companies, to the sole responsibility of marketing and communications. Fortunately, there is an increasing shift inside small and global brands to involve the entire company in the branding process, due to the realities of digital transformation.

By integrating the most effective processes—individuals with expertise and experience, analytics, and digital tools—you will realise ROI now and in the future. Your brand value and marketplace performance will be strengthened in due time.

Making Magic Beyond Launch Day

In a rebranding process, you work to establish your new 'why' or your refined, core purpose. That new 'why' is not just a concept for "Launch Day." Rather, it is a major organisational change that should be translated into employee behaviour and the way you structure your products, services, and everything you do with your brand carriers. It should be reflected in your look and feel within all units of your organisation.

The rollout and on going management does not end with a launch party. In fact, that is when the important next phase begins, Phase 4, Getting It to Last. There are internal teams, external partners, tools, budgets, and more to coordinate. If the effective and important coordination and management of all the key components are not done, that magic, that feeling of who you are and what you want to be as an organisation, will not be optimised to achieve your goals for the brand.

Your brand change is not a quick transformation. It is a longer term process that should be invested in accordingly.

From Multi to Monolithic Brands

Why are so many companies consolidating into one brand? We see companies and other organisations, like hospital groups, moving from a multi to a monolithic brand strategy; moving from a decentralised brand and structure to a centralised one. This might result in benefits in economies of scale, some consolidation of expenses, and strengthening of the marketplace value. However, moving to a monolithic brand structure is not always feasible.

When organisations express their desire to migrate to a monolithic brand, the first question that comes to mind is: Is your company ready for that? If you decide to go to a more centralised strategy, you need to be ready to manage or facilitate that brand from a central core. If you currently have small teams managing the brand in your various geographic locations, or overseeing current sub-brands, are you prepared to form a much larger centralised team organised to do the necessary work? Again, your brand does not stop with the rollout. You have to be ready to implement and manage the brand long-term by allocating the appropriate budget, resources, and planning to do so over time.

> Your brand
> does not stop
> with the rollout

From Consistence to Coherence

We also see that brands are going from consistence to coherence. Consistence could mean the use of the same images and color scheme, even font sizes in specific ways, whilst coherence allows some flexibility with these items, within prescribed ranges.

The building blocks of brands are changing, and we are structuring brand tools and elements into flexible, mix-and-match 'Lego' boxes.

We see brands going from traditional organisations with guidelines they had hoped to enforce for consistency, to one that is a more flexible, kit-of-parts in our age of accelerating digital transformation.

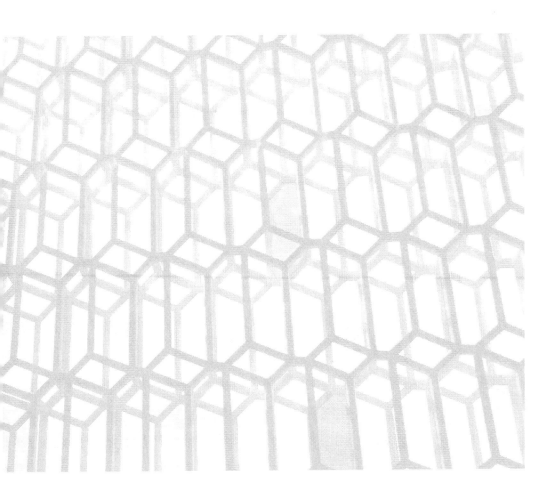

RESOURCES

We have prepared resources at our website for your continued learning: vim-group.com/futureproof

There you will find answers to FAQs, short videos on topics in the book, and downloadable templates to help you with:

- Planning your rebrand
- Estimating your brand change
- Implementing and managing your brand

You will also find access to our upcoming videos and webinars. Sign-up to be notified of our periodic Q+A sessions during which you can get all your questions answered in real-time.

REFERENCES

1. Amazon website. (April 26, 2017). Amazon Go FAQs and video. Retrieved from https://www.amazon.com/b?node=16008589011.

2. Schwab, K. (January 14, 2016). The fourth industrial revolution: What it means, how to respond. Retrieved from https://www.weforum.org/agenda/2016/01/the-fourth-industrial-revolution-what-it-means-and-how-to-respond/.

3. Bhargava, R. (2015). Non-obvious: How to think different, curate ideas, and predict the future. Washington, DC: Ideapress Publishing.

4. TopTrendsUK. (February 24, 2017). The 5G revolution—the internet of things meets everything: Goldman Sachs' Simona Jankowski. [Video]. Retrieved from https://youtu.be/kKQ7Acm-H-g.

5. AT&T. (February 1, 2017). AT&T network 3.0 indigo redefining connectivity through software control, big data and blazing speed. [Press release]. Retrieved from http://about.att.com/story/indigo_redefining_connectivity.html.

6. Ibid.

7. SAP (April 26, 2017). Machine learning microsite. Retrieved from https://www.sap.com/solution/machine-learning.html?url_id=banner-us-homepage-row1-machine-learning-feb17r2.

8. Cisco. (April 26, 2017). IoE—internet of everything for cities states and countries. Retrieved from http://internetofeverything.cisco.com/vas-public-sector-infographic/.

9. Meola, A. (December 19, 2016). What is the internet of things (IoT)? [Blog post]. Retrieved from http://www.businessinsider.com/what-is-the-internet-of-things-definition-2016-8?IR=T.

10. SAP. What is the internet of things (IoT)? [Web page]. Retrieved from https://www.sap.com/solution/internet-of-things.html.

11. Rayala, S. (September 8, 2016). IoT is no future anymore, it is already here. What about IoT in your business? [Blog post]. Retrieved from https://blogs.sap.com/2016/09/08/iot-is-no-future-anymore-it-is-already-here-what-about-iot-in-your-business/.

12. Quoted by Curtin, K. (February 6, 2017). Mixed reality will soon mean big business for brands. [Blog post]. Retrieved from http://venturebeat.com/2017/02/06/mixed-reality-will-soon-mean-big-business-for-brands/.

13. Sheridan, M. (2017). They ask, you answer: A revolutionary approach to inbound sales, content marketing, and today's digital consumer. Hoboken, NJ: John Wiley & Sons, Inc.

14. Fabode, S. (March 10, 2017). 6 technology trends that aren't AI, Blockchain or VR. [Blog post]. Retrieved from https://www.linkedin.com/pulse/6-technology-trends-arent-ai-blockchain-orvr-seyi-fabode?trk=mp-reader-card.

15. Goldman Sachs. (December 13, 2016). Artificial intelligence—the apex technology of the information age: Goldman Sachs' Heath Terry. [Video]. Retrieved from https://youtu.be/zwm2C3V35Fw.

16. Goldman Sachs. (February 2017). David Solomon on the technology landscape. [Video]. Retrieved from http://www.goldmansachs.com/our-thinking/pages/david-solomon-technology-landscape.html.

All other sources are noted within the pertinent text.

MARC CLOOSTERMAN CEO, VIM GROUP

As an experienced and passionate brand consultant to the boardroom, Marc founded VIM Group to develop the discipline of brand implementation and to become a full-fledged business in the marketing and communications sector. Whilst being trained at KPMG and INSEAD, he 'lost his way' two decades ago and began working in marketing, branding, and communications consulting.

During his decades of experience, Marc has personally advised and worked with an extensive list of leading brands, including Airbus Group, Merck, ABB, BMW, TUI Travel, Deloitte, Nordea, Deutsche Telekom, Medtronic, Skoda, and Air Liquide.

His list of professional achievements includes founding the European Association of Communication Directors' Brand Leadership working group and serving on jury panels of various international brand awards programs. He has been a member of supervisory boards of the largest Dutch elderly care organisation and a Swiss-owned media agency. Since 2004, he has been a non-executive director of Brand Finance, the world's leading independent brand valuation consultancy.

Marc speaks three languages (Dutch, English, and German), and he regularly gives talks to practitioners and academics. He has also written extensively about brand implementation and management.

LAURENS HOEKSTRA CSO, VIM GROUP

Laurens founded VIM Group together with Marc. As an experienced business administration and logistics professional, he is an accomplished expert in the brand implementation and management discipline. He was trained at Kuehne & Nagel and INSEAD, a background he has applied to his international work for over twenty years.

With fifteen of those twenty-plus years focused on brands, Laurens is a welcome expert, supporting the boardroom and executive management. That support includes his frequent role as an active part of client steering committees.

Laurens has worked with leading international companies such as Vattenfall, ING Group, SkyTeam, JDE, KPN, IKEA, Air France–KLM, Vopak, NN, Renewi, and Wolters Kluwer. As a result of his invaluable body of knowledge on brand performance, he often delivers lectures about brand implementation and management. Adept at facilitating round table discussions with stakeholder groups, he founded and developed the brand management course in the Netherlands.

In addition to his work at VIM Group, Laurens is an advisory board member of the Big Improvement Day (BIG), a member of the Business Leaders Network, and an ambassador of the Ubuntu Talent Organisation. He is also a tireless mentor to students and coach to several start-up companies.

ABOUT VIM GROUP

VIM Group ensures brands are consistently and coherently delivered around the world. As the category's founder, we bring unrivaled and independent experience and knowledge to various sectors.

Implementation of your brand properties across all touchpoints, both digital and on the ground, is our business.

At VIM Group, we like to do things differently

All too often, different companies in different parts of the world are hired to implement one brand. The results are poor because cross-company coordination is lacking.

The founders of VIM Group decided to establish a new, and much better, way of doing things. We brought the various elements of brand implementation all under one roof in 1991.

As one unified organisation with representatives across the world, VIM Group has robust international, national, and country-specific capabilities. Consultancy, management, and implementation are brought together by a team with a proven track record.

 Delivering your brand promise

Contact

We invite you to learn more about our resources at vim-group.com or get in touch through one of the following modes:

+44 (0)20 7947 4422 or contact@vim-group.com

Please connect with us at our social spaces:

LinkedIn
uk.linkedin.com/company/vim-group

Twitter
twitter.com/vim_group

YouTube
bit.ly/2pnRMqi

Facebook
facebook.com/VIMGroupLtd

We would be happy to welcome you in one of our offices:

UK: London
VIM Group Brand Implementation Ltd.
Warnford Court, 29 Throgmorton Street, London, EC2N 2AT

The Netherlands: Amsterdam
VIM Group Brand Implementation B.V.
Veemarkt 139, 1019 CC Amsterdam

The Netherlands: Hengelo
VIM Group Brand Implementation B.V.
F. Hazemeijerstraat 800, 7555 RJ Hengelo

Germany: Frankfurt am Main
VIM Group Brand Implementation GmbH
Schweizer Straße 9, 60594 Frankfurt am Main

Germany: Munich
VIM Group Brand Implementation GmbH
Luise-Ullrich-Straße 20, 80636 München

20496456R00101

Printed in Poland
by Amazon Fulfillment
Poland Sp. z o.o., Wrocław